This book is a playing guide to successful living and for helpin₁ move forward in their life-jourı

This book is based on the 12 PILARS (Personal Imagery Linked to Active Repetition Socially) cognitive behavioural (CBT) program created by Dr. Alan Curley, PhD PFPH

Dr. Alan Curley is a lecturer in health studies at University of West of Scotland and a Director at UC-MindSolutions Ltd Centre for Sport and life improvement.

Dedicated to:
Past, Present and Future Alan, and all the great games and teams that you have played in, are playing in, and hope to play in the future.

'There must be nothing worse than sitting on your death-bed, replaying your performances and knowing that you played the game of your life completely wrong.
Alan Curley

'When a man has reached his mature age, he can rest at that point of vantage, and cast his eyes back at the long road along which he travelled, lying with its gleams of sunshine and its stretches of shadow in the valley behind him. He can then see its whence and its whither and the twists and bends which were so full of promise or of menace as he approached them,

now lie exposed and open to his gaze. So plain is it all, that he can scarce remember how dark it may have seemed to him or how long he once hesitated at the cross-roads. Therefore, when he tries to recall each stage of the journey, he does so now with the knowledge of its end and thus can no longer make it clear even to himself, how all the pain, worry, heartache, tears, felt like to him at that time......

Modified from 'Uncle Bernac' Sir Arthur Conan Doyle, 1897

Please write any feedback regards this book to
https://www.facebook.com/playingthegameofyourlife
or alan@uc-mindsolutions.com
Or visit www.uc-mindsolutions.com

CHAPTERS

1= The Gambler and the Game
2= My First Summer Sports Camp
3= The Special class of 5
4=Mind Fitness and developing a Game-Mindset
5=What is the purpose of your game?
6= Do you have a Coach with a Game-Mindset?

PILARS Mind Game

7= The Game is afoot, but do you have a map for the journey?- Activating awareness versus Blissful Blindness
8= Where is your desired destination? -Accelerating Ambition versus Anchoring Acceptance
9= Do you want to add more to your Game?-Attitude amplifier versus ambivalence

PILARS Emotional Game

10= Finding focus versus Destroying distraction

11= Manufacturing motivation versus expelling excuses
12= Helpful Beliefs versus unhelpful barriers

PILARS Physical Game
13=Change Commitment versus Change-killers
14= Resilience versus Rejection
15= Results versus Reversors

PILARS Social Game
16= Social bucket changes versus secret results
17= Social resilience versus social rejection
18= Social success versus regretful relapse

19= The Final Game
20= The Journey has ended.

Chapter 1: The Gambler and the Game.

'There must be nothing worse than sitting on your death-bed, replaying your performances and knowing that you played the game of your life completely wrong.
Alan Curley

As I sat on the long train journey home that night, I looked over at the young man sitting across from me and his face seemed familiar. I had saw that look a thousand times on men who had entered my 'Change consultancy' therapy room. It was a look of disenchantment, a look of failed dreams, but most of all a look that said 'how did I manage to end up down here on the substitutes bench', when I thought I would be flying so high in the game.

I asked him his name and he said 'Alan', I could see him strangely looking at my kilted outfit and so I told him, that I was traveling home after being at a Sports awards dinner that night as I was a friend of 'Rocky Richards'. He looked impressed at my blatant name-dropping and so I offered him a glass of my wine, which I had rather cheekily procured at the awards ceremony (well it was a £100 bottle of the finest vino which would have went to waste if I hadn't heroically rescued it).

He told me that the game of life had given him some tough decisions recently and he now realized that it would take some big, difficult changes to turn the result of his game around. He told me truthfully that he wasn't even sure if he had the skill, energy or time left to be able to make the changes. He did not appreciate my wry smile as I said that maybe he should look for a smaller, easier changes to try instead. He then sighed and told me that he wished he could go back in time and try and find out where it all went wrong, to speak to his younger self, and try to convince him to make some different decisions. His words made me recall my favourite scene from the film **'The**

Shawshank redemption', where the character goes in for his parole hearing.

In order to break up the long train journey home, then I asked him if he wanted to play cards, but he said that he had no money, so I replied that we would play for our 'life-Goals' instead. The game of poker was something I was very good at, due to my trained ability to read people and the true meaning of their words and facial expressions, and therefore predict accurately what their next move would be. By the time, we finished playing the last game of the night, the young man asked me if I was a professional gambler, mainly due to the fact that he was running out of 'life-Goals' to play me with.

Laughing I turned to him and in a very **'Kenny rogers-esque' way, I said, 'son I am no gambler, but I have 'made my living from reading people's faces and behaviours and knowing what their cards were, by the way they held their eyes, and if you don't mind me saying, I can see your out of aces, so let me give you some advice'.**

I told him, that I thought 'Life is like a game', but most people don't even know they are playing in it, and the ones that do know they are playing, often do not know what the rules of their game are, or what they have to do to win it. Furthermore, very few people seem to know what the best strategies are, for making sure that they play their game to their full potential, and thus give themselves the best chance of winning their game and being part of a winning team. It often seemed to me, that **most people spent more time working out how their mobile phone works, than spending it on working out how their mind and emotions and behaviours work in the game of their life.**

I went back into Kenny-Rogers mode and told him that 'every good gambler knows their game well'. They know that every hand can be a winner and every hand can be a loser, but the key to gambling success is knowing what cards to throw away and when, whilst deciding wisely, on which hands to keep because they are worth developing.

My last piece of advice to him, was that if he wants to keep playing in the game of his life, then he better learn to play it right. Next thing I remember, was finding myself smiling as I hummed the immortal lyrics of **Kenny rogers song 'the gambler'. 'You got to know when to hold them, know when to fold them, Know when to walk away and know when to run, you never count your money when your sitting at the table, there will be time enough for counting, when the dealing is done',** and the game has ended.

He had noticed that I was still glancing periodically at my laptop and as he looked Down at my computer, asked me if I was playing blackjack, I smiled and said" no, I am genuinely not a professional gambler". I told him that I was playing a game which a university colleague of mine had created years ago. It was a kind of mind-training, decision-enhancing therapy game. You play as an avatar who is a therapist and whose clients are in different problem life-scenarios. Each player is then given choices of different things you can get your client to say, or think or to do, in order to try and help them change and feel happier or become more successful. Whichever player gets their clients the biggest increase in score of their happiness and success levels, wins the game.

With pride I told him, that My ability to read people's thoughts and behaviours had grown even more acutely over time, due in part to playing it, and I was now considered one of the best players in the game.

The game I said, 'is also used for helping young people improve their decision making skills as they can keep playing the same scene and see all the different consequences or rewards to the various different decisions that their avatar makes. It is also used in prison rehabilitation centres for helping inmates to see that there are other behaviour options often available for altering your emotions or dealing with anger and frustration better.

Finally, it has been used with people who attempted suicide to help them work through alternative solutions to helping them with their problems. It has also been used with the loved ones who still suffer the trauma of having lost someone to suicide, but who still blame themselves for not noticing any signs or symptoms. I told him that many people have found comfort in this game as it can work through issues and find alternative virtual solutions which they never had a chance to do in the real world with their loved one.

Noticing that he looked lost and low in hope, then I asked him to try and play the game for himself. I thought it may help him to try and work out alternative strategies for his current life issues and help him find another solution, rather than the one that we both knew he had come on the train to make.

I was happy that 'Alan', seemed to engage with the computer game, and while he kept playing at it on my laptop, then my mind began to drift slowly back to that nights earlier festivities.

I vividly travelled back to hours earlier, when I was sitting at the awards ceremony table, dressed in my kilt getting more happy with each glass of wine.

I remember feeling completely honoured to be part of the glamour and prestige of this years 'National sports academy awards.

It was no secret who the next winner was, but still I smiled as they announced to the stage that the winner of this years 'life-time hall of fame' award was Rocky 'Resilient' Richards. The most successful midfielder in football over the last 30 years. The cameras quickly panned over to his table and sitting alongside me was a few other old familiar faces. There was, Lennon 'the Joker', and 'Paulo the Philospher' and 'Anxious' Ishmal.

Rocky's family were all at the table and I admit, that I was a little envious, as I could see the looks of love and respect from his beautiful wife, and four Children, as well as all the other members of this elite audience who stood clapping his famed sporting success.

Little did they know of the young Rocky, that I once met. Even Rocky's past self, would have been astounded at this future star and all the success he had achieved in the game of Football. He had played at the highest professional level and made shed-loads of money. Even after his playing career had ended, he became a great youth coach, and then the most successful team manager of all-time. Even to this day, he was still going strong as a much loved 'pundit' of the game on satellite TV, and to cap it all off, he was one of the Directors of the most successful club (which he helped build) in Britain.

Many of the accolades that he received from other people that night, repeated a familiar theme about his ability to maximise his own potential, as well as the potential of others In the game and to keep consistently developing and diversifying himself to every new challenge, that this beautiful game had threw at him, with a resilience and attitude that was unsurpassed.

Little did they all know, that it was this 'Old Professor', who had helped guide him on his journey to great game success.

When he finally received the 'lifetime hall of fame' award and spoke at the podium, I was humbled to hear him mention my name and 'Plug' my book called **'The PILARS of Mind Fitness and developing a Game mindset',** which had sat dusty on the shelf for many a year now. It was no surprise for me, to hear him speak with purpose and passion about his memories in the game and admit heartfelt gratitude to all those team-members, who had helped him on his journey to 'Perfecting' his game. I would have expected nothing less from my former student.

What did surprise many people though, was the way, that he constantly alluded to his 'past-selves', whom he wished to thank most of all, for it was their sacrifice, pain, time, energy, belief, focus, motivation, resilience and hard-work, which had given him the life and success and happiness that he had today.

I grinned as I saw the strange looks from the crowd as he kept thanking his past-selves, it was obvious from their confused response, that they had not read my book.

Finally, when the ceremony had ended, we were whisked off to a lavish hotel in the city and after many drinks and many drunken toasts later, there was only the 5 of us left, Myself, Rocky, Lennon, Paulo and Ishmal. As we all sat beside the hotel fireside, I proceeded to hand over my 'Gift' to Rocky, as a thank you, for the wonderful invite to his 'crowning glory night'.

The gift was something that I knew, even with all his wealth that he could not buy. It was the research report that I had written many years before, about the 5 young footballers who attended my first ever 'Mind fitness' program at a 12 week 'Summer Sports Performance Improvement Academy'.

This report outlined my predictions of how I thought, they would all perform in their future games, after having spent 12 weeks of training them in **The PILARS of Mind Fitness and developing a Game mindset'.**

I could see from the astonished looks in their eyes, that they all had wondered for many years, about the predictions that I had written in my report about them. I got the feeling, that each of them had spent many moments agonizing over whether I had accurately predicted their future-fortunes on how they would perform in their game.

It was on this special night that I had decided to share the secrets of my report with them.

My report was called' The 12 PILARS of the Game Journey'.

Chapter 2: My first Summer Sports camp-

'What is Predictable is preventable'.
Alan Curley

The Train stopped and my mind wandered back to reality when 'Alan' leaned over and asked me 'how did I know 'Rocky Richards'?
I laughed and asked him, 'how long did he have left on his journey as it was a long-story', he smiled and said 'he still had a few hours to go'. So, as he continued to play my mind training decision enhancing computer game on the laptop, then I began to tell him the story of how I met the 'Great Rocky Richards', and the 12 weeks I spent with him in summer camp many years ago.
I told him that this story and that computer game might just help him move forward again on his own journey in the Game.

So I began the story with, 'I will never forget the day, that I turned up at my very first 12 week 'Summer Sports Performance Improvement Academy'.
Earlier that year, I had wrote a book called **"The PILARS of Mind Fitness and developing a Game mindset'**, which had earned me some Media acclaim. This was because I had used the theories within the book, when working with some professional sportspeople and they had all went on to perform to their personal best ever and win against the odds. These career best performances, had then caught the attention of the sports media and they had written a series of articles on my work.
The idea of using cognitive behaviour change theories to 'help people beat their addictions', had been widely acknowledged and accepted in medicine and healthcare for many years now. However, my adaptation of these addiction techniques and theories, for use in the Professional sports arena to 'help

people beat their opponents', by improving their mind fitness, had been generally met with a lot of scorn and disbelief.

Nonetheless there were a few coaches and Sporting visionaries who had contacted me after reading my book, as they were convinced that it could help young athletes develop their 'mind fitness and game mindset', which would help them to improve and reach their potential in the game. One of these coaches and sporting visionaries was Frank Ferrell, a large ex-professional England Goalkeeper who now ran the "Summer Sports Performance Improvement Academy', for some of the most gifted young footballers in England aged 16 years Old.

Frank had written to me a few months earlier and invited me to attend the summer camp this year in Oxford, as a 'Guest training coach'. Normally, the opportunity to work with teenagers, would be something that I would have avoided like a viral infection. However, there was something that Frank had mentioned in his email, which made this particular group of young players, who had signed up this summer, very special indeed.

I couldn't believe my luck, when I re-read his email, as this would fit perfectly with a research proposal, that I had recently secured funding from the United Kingdom Sports Research Council (UKSRC) to undertake. After years of brow-beating them, then the UKSRC had finally agreed to help financially support me in my bid to test and prove the success of the theories and techniques, which I had written about in my book entitled, **"The PILARS of Mind Fitness and developing a Game mindset'.**

Furthermore, the five-figure fee that Frank had offered me, along with the chance to go back and spend the summer in Oxford, where I had previously studied, was in the words of the Godfather, **'Simply an offer I couldn't refuse'.**

I quickly wrote back to Frank, agreeing to his proposal. I had no idea at this point in time, just how important this group of 5 young players would be to the future history of 'Sports Psychology, mind fitness, game-mindset and helping young players to reach their potential in the game'.

Frank, took me to the coaches staffroom and introduced me to the other 5 summer camp coaches, as 'Professor Curley, the mind fitness and game performance-doctor', which unsurprisingly, did not get me off to a good start with them.

It was obvious that they were all from athletic sporting backgrounds and were not too impressed with the small, scrawny, academic Scotsman, who was here to teach their young English sporting prodigies, about how to use their minds to become mentally fitter and play their game better.

I then received the usual jokes about 'good luck finding some of these young players brains, let alone enhance them'. I laughed in response to their quips, to try and help create a connection with them.

At this point in the coach's staffroom, I felt like the tokenistic minority ethnic player who is selected to appear in the team just to comply with equality and diversity laws.

In fairness though, Frank went on to tell the other coaches with great earnest, that he firmly believed in my work and wanted to give these potential football stars of the future, the chance to get coached in their mental fitness and game mindset. This was an area of their performance, that no footballer of previous generations had been allowed the opportunity to try and develop.

The 12 week summer football camp was set-up as follows, There were 22 of England's finest young football talent at the camp. They were evenly split into two teams, A and B.

Each group would sit in various training and coaching sessions every day until the Sunday of each week. Then on the Sunday, Team A and Team B would play against each other. The aim would be, that they would now use the additional skills that they had learned that week in their sessions, to test which team and which players were improving the most.

Every Sunday, after they played their football match, then each of the young players would be assessed by the coaches and points would be awarded to each player based on their level of performance in the game. At the end of the 12 weeks, there would be a prize given to the player who scored the most points overall, as well as a prize given to the player who had most improved their performance over the 12 weeks. However, there was a bigger prize to play for and the boys all knew it, for on the last day of the 12 week camp, both teams would play a final match against each other, in front of Premiership football team scouts, who were looking to sign up junior talent to the professional ranks of the top English league.

There were 5 other coaches who took daily sessions with the full squad of 22 young men these were:

Pete- The strength and conditioning coach

Ian-Cardiovascular fitness coach

Larry- The football Skills coach

Andy- The football Physiotherapy coach

Rob-The Sports Nutritionist

and finally, Frank the head coach, who taught the young players all about strategies, formations and tactics within the game.

My role was different though, as I had only agreed to coach at this summer camp, if I was allowed to work with 5 specific young players, whom I had instantly selected when I first read Franks original email. The idea of the research project, was that I would work with these 5 players in a special class, where they would learn all about the 12 PILARS of 'Mind fitness' which I had written about in my book, **"The PILARS of Mind Fitness and developing a GAME mindset'**. Then at the end of the 12 weeks, we would test whether these 5 players had improved on their game, more than any of the other young players at the camp (who had not attended my class). This test would be carried out by comparing the scores given to these 5 players from my class each week by the other 5 coaches, who were also assessing the performances of each of the 22 boys, every week when they played their Sunday game.

Now I hear you ask, what was so special about these 5 young players that had made me instantly agree to coach them at this summer-camp?

Well, each of them was an identical twin, and their identical siblings were also at the camp.

Each of the 5 boys which I had selected to be in my 'special class', was considered to be equally as good at playing the game as their identical twin, who was also at the camp, but who would not be part of my 'special' class.

I couldn't believe my luck when I had first read Franks email telling of the strange fact that for the first time ever, out of the 22 boys selected to attend this summer camp, that there was 5 sets of identical twins within the squad (I had wondered if this was something to do with the high incidence of IVF fertility treatment available to their parent's generation).

To me, this was a gift from the research gods, as I had previously spent time at the Twin unit at St. Thomas's hospital in London, and it was clear to me, that in order to test if my 12 'PILARS' of mind-fitness', would enhance the gaming mindset and performance in one set of subjects versus another set of placebo subjects, then I needed to eliminate as many other variables as possible. Therefore, the opportunity to work with identical twins at this summer camp, would reduce so many of these other irritable research variables like age, genetics, developmental environment, diet, parenting, social class, peer-influence and education. Thus, finally giving me the chance to prove to the Sporting world, that my 12 PILARs of mind fitness, could improve any players overall performance in the game.

As I sat that first day, at the initial coaches meeting, barely listening to Frank, because my mind was still racing with research joy, there was one final conversation which strangely caught my ear.

To my amazement, the tradition each year, was that the coaches would take part in a betting game linked to each of the 22 young players at the camp called 'fantasy football league'.

This fantasy league game, consisted of writing on a board which hung up in the coaches staffroom wall, each of the 22 young players names, and in a column beside each name was written what each of the young players current 'potential money value' was rated at (strangely enough, this had already been produced by the financial accountants at each of their football clubs, in order to protect the clubs investment in these young players). In the final blank column, would be written how many total points they would have earned throughout their 12 Sunday football games that they would play at summer camp. Just like a fantasy football league, the idea was that each coach was given '**100 million pounds**' of 'fantasy' money to spend and they had to 'buy' the 11 young players that they thought would earn the most points over the next 12 weeks. Points awarded in the game could be positive or negative and were based on certain criteria. For example, positive scores were given for scoring a goal, assisting someone else to score a goal, gaining a penalty for your team, saving a goal or assisting in stopping a goal.

Negative scores were given for giving away a penalty, getting sent off, or allowing your marker to score.

This was an interesting concept to me, as I thought the idea that coaches and football clubs, could 'predict the potential future value and worth' in footballers so young, was surely a very foolish thing to do.

As it turned out, I was wrong.

Chapter 3: The Special class of 5

When the students are ready, then the teacher will arrive'.
Anon

When I first entered the class to teach this special group of 5 gifted footballers, I was totally underwhelmed by them and their initial slow response of 'hello sir'.

However, one of them did stand out from the crowd, his wry smile and natural confidence along with his cool rebel-like stature, and strutting proud walk, made me instantly realise that this must be Aldous 'The peacock' Allan.

It didn't take me long to guess who the other 4 boys were also, firstly, there was 'Lennon the joker' Ludbeck, standing next to him was 'Paulo the Philosopher' Peters, next to him was 'Anxious Ishmal Ingram' and finally sitting down was 'Rocky Resilient Richards'.

You see, I had already been given a summary report of each of the 5 boys, created from all the statements that their previous coaches had written about them. They were as follows:

Paulo 'The Philosopher' Peters: He played as a Centre-back.
Paulo, came from a religious, hard working-class family. He and his twin, were the oldest of 4 children.

His parents attended every match and were very strict with him. He was a quiet, intelligent boy who did well at school. He was known for sometimes over-thinking the game and not playing enough in it (hence why he was nicknamed the philosopher).

He was good at always listening to coaches and taking instructions well. He played the ball very safe and never took risky chances or tried to gain glory for himself. A good solid consistent team player.

Positive traits=

Big, strong tough player, very good tackler of the ball, and keeps to his role in the team. Hard-working, takes instruction well from experienced superiors, safe and dependable with very little risky play, always agrees with and tries to please the coach.

Negative traits=

Lacks some self-belief and confidence. He often won't push himself forward in the game, in case he gets a decision wrong. He sometimes lacks passion and flair playing in his game. He doesn't' adapt quickly or well with a change of tactics at half-time in the game and needs everything explained to him beforehand.

He was rated by his current football club (and therefore also in the coaches fantasy football league chart) as a player of potential future value = £15 million pounds.

Ishmal 'Anxious' Ingram= He played at Left-back.

Ishmal, was from a poor background. He was from a single-parent family, as his father was an alcoholic and had left his mother a few years ago. Although every so often his father would appear back into their lives normally causing problems for Ishmal , his twin and his mother. His mother did not attend any of his games.

He was very tall and athletic, but coaches and had noted that he often lacked fitness for the full-game and would often get worried and distracted and make mistakes in the last 30 minutes of each game. His nickname 'anxious' came from the fact he was a worrier and always assumed something negative would happen in the game.

Positive traits=

Tall and athletic with a fast turn of pace, has natural ability with the ball, but lacks confidence with it.

Negative traits=

He was not as fit as he should be, can give up too easily when a game gets tough, does not communicate at all on the pitch with his team-mates. He is a poor decision-maker when put under pressure with the ball and doesn't often understand team tactics and can keep making the same mistakes. He can get upset when given criticism of this by coaches and is easily led by other negative characters in the team. Lacks drive and ambition on the pitch and can appear too contented with losing. He can be over-critical of coaches and other players and will often see the negative aspect of strategies.

He was rated by his current football club (and therefore also in the coaches fantasy football league chart) as a player of future value = £1 million pounds.

Lennon 'The Joker' Ludbeck= He played on the Right-wing.
Lennon, was from a working class background. Him and his twin, were the youngest children of 2 half-sisters, a half-brother and 2 brothers. His parents often attended his games, but were often sent away from the games by the referee, due to bad language and aggressive touch-line behavior. Lennon is a very funny and likeable dressing room character (hence his nickname 'the joker'), who enjoys his football. He is small, quick and plays with no fear. He has a powerful left-shot, but often lacks vision and concentration and awareness in the game. Can also lose his temper too easily and is prone to being sent-off.

Positive traits=
Quick with the ball, good first-touch and good striker of the ball, loyal and hard-working for his coach and team-mates, plays with no fear, a lot of stamina and will play to the end. A good positive dressing-room character.

Negative traits=
He can get distracted and lose focus too easily, which makes him lose the ball to other players. His play can be inconsistent and undisciplined. This lack of focus, often leads to a loss in his temper and he can easily be wound-up by opposition players to get sent-off. Has a poor second-touch of the ball and can lack ability and vision to know when to pass to other team-mates. Can be slow in the timing of his challenges and finds it difficult to switch his play, especially when games are tough. He takes feedback well from coaches, but often does not seem to be

able to turn it into action. He does not take the big games or competitions seriously enough and prefers to be the Joker off and on the pitch and often at the wrong times in the game.

He was rated by his current football club (and therefore also in the coaches fantasy football league chart) as a player of future value = £5 million pounds.

Aldous "The Peacock" Allan=   **He played as an attacking midfielder and striker.**

Aldous and his twin brother were considered equally to be the best players at the camp and potential future England stars. They were from a wealthy self-made family. Aldous and his twin, attended a private school and had no other siblings. His parents had split up when he was young, but he was still spoiled with many gifts and tokens of their love. He was tall, strong, quick, powerful and therefore naturally gifted at most things sporty. He was highly competitive, rebellious and a born winner who did not like losing. Finally, he was very confident and had the looks and style of a catalogue model, with a winning wry smile, that attracted a lot of female admirers to his game. Often it was him, who was the match-winner for his team-mates and he thoroughly enjoyed rejoicing in the glory of his past successes. His nickname 'The Peacock', came for the natural way he strutted on and off the pitch with a natural confident air of arrogance and superiority.

Positive traits=

Strong, quick, confident and powerful with the ball, has natural two-footed skill and ability, fast turn of pace and highly competitive, with great skill at dribbling, shooting and heading the ball, as well as a cool, calm, quick decisive finisher in front of goal. The boy had it all.

Negative traits=

Often plays for himself and his glory, rather than as a team player. His tactics can be very selfish in the game and he will often not pass to other team-mates, even if they have a better chance of scoring a goal. Does not keep as fit or work as hard as he should for the team, and will often play worse, lose focus, stop trying and become disruptive when things are not going his way or the game appears lost. He can be impulsive and take needless risks in the game, in order to go for personal glory, these risks often lead to bad decisions and results for the team. He can often appear to think he is superior to his team-mates and therefore expects his team-mates to work harder for him. Thus, he often relies on other players to bail him out of mistakes and trouble in the game. He does not like sharing the glory when other team-mates play well and he can appear jealous when others get man of the match.

He has a habit of not listening to the coach's tactics and can appear that he thinks that he knows better, which means that he does not seek the help of others with his development in the game. He does not take criticism well and shrugs off feedback or argues with it, which means he never takes any responsibility for a team-loss .

He was rated by his current football club (and therefore also in the coach's fantasy football league chart) as a player of future value = £30 million pounds.

Rocky 'Resilient' Richards = He played as a Central holding midfielder.

Rocky and his twin had been adopted by a middle-class family. His parents were very supportive and often helped out in an active role at the clubs he played for as well as in his education. He was polite, humble and intelligent.

He was competitive and wiry, with a great vision for a pass and great balance in his style of play. A great motivator and strong team player, who could adapt his play quickly and well, whether his team were winning or losing (hence his nickname 'Resilient').

Positive traits=

Had average skill, but great fitness, work rate and stamina. A great passer of the ball, with good vision and awareness of tactics and intelligent strategies against opponents. He can plan and deliver set-plays well and is a good crosser of the ball. He has great balance and takes strong challenges well. He can switch play when needed. He is organized, confident, a good decision-maker and communicator on the field and will include and motivate other players who 'are missing in action' in the game. He is competitive and ambitious and listens well to the coach's advice. He sets high expectations and goals for his own performance as well as the team's performance in the game.

Negative traits=

Does not score enough goals and could be more of an assertive leader and critical of other team players when in the dressing-room. Tries to please others in the team and is often very self-critical and will take full blame and responsibility for a poor team performance. He could be more physical in his game and could be more impulsive and quicker in his decisions in front of the goal. He could be more confident and needs to be more selfish on the pitch, as he will often give up good chances in front of goal, to allow others to try and score.

He was rated by his current football club (and therefore also in the coach's fantasy football league chart) as a player of future value = £10 million pounds.

After I had read all the summary reports for each of the 'special 5' boys, then I was amazed to read very similar descriptions when I read over their twin's reports. Their footballing similarities seemed to be as identical as their Physical similarities. Furthermore, their predicted future value, placed on them by the football club accountants were identical also.

This made me wonder, 'whether the true future worth of any player, is purely and simply linked to their genetics'?

This made me remember that I once heard someone say, 'You can't change the place where you were born or the hand that you were dealt in the game',

but I did wonder, 'can you?'

Chapter 4: Mind Fitness & developing a Game Mindset

"We do not stop playing because we grow old, we grow old because we stop playing".
Benjamin Franklin

Although I had given many lectures on **'The PILARS of Mind Fitness and developing a Game mindset'**, I was feeling strangely nervous, as this was the first time, that I would be delivering the 12 week program to a class of teenagers.

I tried to remember some of the classic tips when addressing a new or difficult audience, like Start with a joke or ice-breaker. I then proceeded to check that the computer and IT equipment were not going to make a complete fool out of me in front of these tech-savvy teenagers.

Finally, I arranged in alphabetical order, each of the boy's folders which contained their class notes and images, as well as their homework exercises for the next 12 weeks. I kept repeating my positive mantra, 'This project **will be fun**, you are not feeling nervous, those feelings you are having are ones of **excitement**, in order to try and convince myself to start believing it.

The boys all arrived together for the introductory session of my course and all of them sat on in the row of chairs at the back of the class. I pondered on why no-one ever sits in the front row chairs, maybe it is a mental scar from being picked on by the teacher at school, or not wanting to look over-enthusiastic, or maybe people think that just like a comedian, you will highlight and poke fun at anyone, whose sitting in front of stage.

When they settled down, I introduced myself as 'Professor Curley', and explained to them why they had been separated into this special group of 5 players.

Aldous shouted 'yes thanks for that sir', as we are now known at camp as the 'Special 5', and then he proceed to elongate the word 's-p-e-c-i-a-l', in a very derogatory way.

My aim here I said, is to 'help you improve your mind fitness and develop a better game-mindset'. 'This will help you to go on and physically play the best potential game that you have in you'. 'This means introducing you to mind-fitness coaching, which helps you to perform to your optimal physical skill and then consistently play at this optimal level, no matter what game situation that you find yourself in, or what challenges that you receive, or which opponent you find yourself standing in front of'.

I could see by their reactions, that they were not convinced about this 'Mind fitness and game mindset' nonsense.

So, I asked them if they all agreed, 'that it was common for people to admit to others, that they are not as physically fit as they have been before, or could be, but that they are trying to get themselves physically fitter'. Furthermore, most people are happy to share with others, that they have hired a personal fitness coach, who is helping them devise a program which will get them fitter as quickly as possible and gain whatever physical transformation that they are looking for. It seems to me like everyone is happy and willing to acknowledge, that at different times in their life, their physical fitness levels have changed and that sometimes their physical fitness, has been less than it is just now and at the other times their physical fitness has been greater than it is just now. Next, I asked them, if they would also agree, that there are other footballers more physically fit than them and some less so, but that you don't worry about their levels of fitness, you just keep trying to improve your own fitness levels, because if you can improve your fitness levels, then you can improve on how well your playing in the game. I then asked them if they accepted, that if you go to a gym and keep training, then your physical fitness levels will go up and if you don't train for a while then your physical fitness levels will go down. However, because your physical fitness levels are changeable, then you can always bring your fitness levels back up, by going back into the gym and spending more time and energy working on your training again.

Finally, I asked if they agreed that when your physical fitness levels go down, then you cannot perform as well in the game.

They all seemed extremely bored already with my long list of statements, but they seemed to agree with these statements, because I heard the low grunting of teenage murmurs from the back of the class.

Well I said, if you are happy to admit those truths about your physical fitness, and we all agree that the mind and body are connected, then why do people still have a stigma about admitting that they are exactly the same principles for your mind fitness levels also.

People should feel comfortable to admit to others, that they are not as mentally-fit as they have been before, or could be, and so they are currently trying to get themselves mentally fitter. People should be happy to share with others, that they have hired a mind fitness coach, who is helping them devise a program which will get them mentally fitter as quickly as possible and gain whatever mindset transformation that they are looking for. Furthermore, it is okay to admit that at certain times of our life, other people have different levels of mind fitness to us, but we shouldn't be focused on whether they are mentally fitter than us, but rather we should just keep trying to increase our own mind fitness levels. People should accept, that there will be times in your life when you are mentally fitter than at other times. For example if we have periods away from own mind training, because we have had to deal with other life-issues, then this will lower our mind's fitness levels, but we can always increase our levels of mind fitness by spending the time and energy back into it and working on our training. Finally, when our mind fitness levels go down, then we cannot perform as well, but if we can learn to increase the fitness levels of our mind, then we will improve how well we can perform again in our game, which may help us to start scoring goals again.

Boys, 'the aim of this 12 week class, is to help you learn to master your 'mental and emotional state' during the game. This will also help to increase your resilience levels, to quickly and effectively adapt yourself to any Physical, emotional and Social changes which occur in your game'.

The techniques I will coach you in, over the next 12 weeks, can help you to maximise your focus and awareness levels during the game, in order to improve your decision-making abilities. Finally, this program will help you learn the most efficient ways to spend your skill, energy and time during the game, so that you and your team can score even more goals (or give less goals away to the opposition).

This may sound easy I said, but believe me guys, 'It is easier said than done'.

But if you all listen and work with me, then I promise that I can definitely help coach you to get mentally fitter and develop a better game-mindset. This I can guarantee you, will help you to play your game better and score more goals and achieve more wins for your team', that is of course, only if you genuinely wish to improve your game.

Aldous then shouted from the back, 'Professor, does that mean you can guarantee me, that I will now score a hat-trick in every football game and go on to beat Michael Mumfords all-time record of 120 fantasy football points which he gained at this summer camp 10 years ago.

I smiled as I looked back at his 'gallus expression' and whispered quietly back to the whole class, **'Who said that I was talking about helping you to play the game of football better'?**

Chapter 5: What is the purpose of your Game?

The meaning of life is to find your gift, the purpose of life is to give it away'.
Pablo Picasso

I had never forgotten about the stages of a great lecture, Firstly, pose the audience a question?

So, I asked the boys this: 'If an alien came down to earth and asked you 'What is the purpose of your game and How does your team win the game', what would you tell it?

Aldous quickly replied with a little scorn in his voice "SIMPLES sir,' I would say to it, 'by scoring more goals than you give away'.

They all giggled like schoolgirls and then looked at me strangely when I said,

'I guess your simply right Aldous', 'You do need to score more Goals and achieve more victories, than you give away', in order to win.

What if the Alien then wanted to know, 'What was the purpose of your specific role or position in the game"? what would you tell it?'

Aldous quickly shouted out again 'My role as striker, is to score lots of goals and to gain the feelings of joy and pleasure, knowing that I helped my team win'.

I said, 'brilliant Aldous, but what if you're a defender'?

Paulo, the defender quietly said, 'my purpose in the team is 'To not give away goals and to avoid the feelings of pain and discomfort, knowing that you helped your team lose', they all laughed, but were silenced when I said, 'that this was another great answer'.

Then I asked Rocky the midfielder, what the purpose of his role was, as he was neither a striker nor a defender and he said 'to control the ball well and decide how best to distribute it, in order to support the other players in the team', I basically, help take the pressure off defenders from losing goals, whilst I assist the strikers to score their goals'. Excellent answer Rocky, I proclaimed.

So, what you are telling me boys is that

'If you change the position you play in the game, then this will change your view on your role within the team, and thus change your focus on what goal is now important for you to achieve in the game?

'Precisely' said Ishmal (he had been very quiet up to this point).

Before I gave them their first class assignment, then I wanted them to ponder over this question: 'What if the alien now asked you 'How do you know, if you have played well in your game?".

They looked at me like I was going slowly mad.

So I tried to explain by saying **'well, like most of the games in your life, you won't actually know if you are happy with your performance and feel that you played well, unless you had an idea of what you hoped to achieve before the game started'.**

'So on that rather topical note', I said 'your first class assignment', which you have 15 minutes to complete, (I could now here the growing grunts of dissatisfaction emanating from the back of the room, from the news that they were having to do some work) is this:'.

Assignment 1

Your assignment I said, is to 'imagine that you have just retired from professional football and Sky sports are writing a column and producing a documentary about your playing career.

I now want you to imagine everything that you hope will be written or said about you and your achievements in the game, in this retirement documentary'. To help them with this I played them the song, 'I wanna be adored', by the Stone roses. I hoped that the music would help them think more.

In your assignment you should write and record a video of the following answers to these 5 statements:

1=List all the major achievements and successes that you hope to have won in your time in the game? and What is the 1 most important thing that you want to have achieved and be remembered for?
2=What do you think your team-mates would say about your strengths & weaknesses within the team?
3=How many great friends did you make in the game and why were they great friends?
4=What do you wish that you had done more of and less of, with the time you spent in the game?
5=What do you hope to do, now that you have finished playing the game?

After, the 15minutes had elapsed, then I asked the boys how they had got on with their video.

Aldous had not really done it, as he knew he just wanted to win the world cup and that was it, he didn't care about anything else, as nothing else was as important in the game.

However, the other 4 boys had made decent enough attempts at a short retirement video documentary and I really enjoyed listening to the youthful hopes and aspirations in each of their videos. Rocky had made the most detailed and specific attempt of honestly but ambitiously recording what he hoped to hear about his achievements at the end of his playing career. So, I gave him the highest score for his assignment.

As I watched their retirement videos, it reminded me, of why I enjoyed talking to young players in the game, as they always had so many wonderful and exciting goals and ambitions that they genuinely believed they would achieve in their future. However, the problem that I saw, was that only a few of them ever seemed to make it anywhere near the potential, that their younger self had aspired and hoped for. I wondered to myself what cruelly happens along life's path, that turns the journey of energetic, optimistic, ambitious, idealistic teenagers into tired, cynical, unambitious mid-life beings.

Most of them seem to lose their ability, to keep developing at a rate which is required to reach that professional or successful level in the game, which their younger self believed that they would achieve.

I often wondered, 'Was it because their coaches were not good enough at developing them beyond the amateur level in the game', or was it just that 'they ultimately, did not have the innate skills, that their younger selves thought that they had, in order to make it to the professional level?

I had read a sad statistic the previous week in Sports Psychology monthly, where research had shown that 90% of sportspeople who had the serious potential to make it to a professional level in their game, had prematurely stopped developing their own professional talent and career, in order to accept work in junior coaching roles. This had been shown to be true in Football, baseball, athletics, gymnastics, Tennis, Golf, basketball, Boxing, Martial Arts, and Rugby.

This fact made me remember the words of John Lennon, **'life is what happens to you, whilst your busy making other plans'**, although I did think maybe he was wrong and it should have been, **'life will happen to you, unless you get busy making other plans'**.

Chapter 6: Do you have a coach with a Game-Mindset?

A coach is someone who can give correction without causing resentment."
John Wooden

In the next class, I decided to alter the seating arrangements because the boys had previously sat in a row at the very back away from me. So, I rearranged the chairs into an open circle. When the boys finally came in and sat down, then I noticed, there was a strange solemn atmosphere In the room. I asked the boys 'what was wrong', and they all looked over at Ishmal with concern.

I asked Ishmal if he wanted to share his issue with the group.

He proceeded to tell me that, every Saturday the boys were given the day off, to go into town and do what they wished (within reason of course).

This week Ishmal had met up with his dad. However, his father had appeared with a drink in him and had got angry and violent with Ishmal, telling the boy that his attitude towards his performances in the game so far, was not good enough. He had shouted to Ishmal, that this was his only chance of success and that he better not screw it up or he would feel his father's punishment, and probably end up serving fries at macdonalds for the rest of his life.

Ishmal, had since been getting more upset and anxious that his dad was correct and now he was worried about 'messing' up the next 12 weeks of camp and never making it as a good football player in the game.

I could see that Ishmal was deeply upset at the abusive encounter with his father, but strangely enough, the other boys were being uncharacteristically kind and supportive towards him (I guess some of them had also experienced this kind of negative abusive pressure before). It was a nice scene for me to see, as I watched these boys drop their macho-image for a brief moment and show genuine care and compassion towards their team-mate. Although in fairness, their well-meant but unhelpful supportive words of delivering retribution on his father, did not seem to be helping Ishaml, and I could clearly see that he was still focusing on his dads fears coming true and not focused on his own goals instead.

To try and distract the focus away from Ishmal, then I said to the boys, ' Do you remember explaining to the alien in the first session that the rule of winning the game is to 'To score more Goals than you give away'. And that your role in winning this team game can either be to 'defend against losing goals, or to support others to score goals, or to score the goals yourself.
Therefore, in this session, the alien has another question to ask you about your game?
'Who did you learn the rules of the game from, and how do you know if you are meant to be a defender, midfielder or striker in the game'?
My question was met with puzzled looks, just like a therapist asking a depressed patient, how they know 'that they are depressed'?
The boys shrugged their shoulders and said in unison, 'the coach taught us the rules, and then figured out what our best position is, based on the skills we have'.
So I asked, 'But what if you were always just out playing with a ball in the street with your friends, and you never had a coach to tell you the rules, or what your skills and best position were'?
Aldous's reply was almost instant, 'Well without a coach and not knowing the rules, then you would never be able to get any good at the game or manage to develop the skills you need to help you win a game'.
'Yes, I guess you would Aldous', I replied, Rocky then laughed and added, 'yeah, it would just be like playing football the way we did when we were young, before we were in an organised team with a coach'. 'Do you remember, we would all just run around every day in a large group, tiring ourselves out by chasing the ball aimlessly up and down the street, trying to play

all positions, and not even knowing who was on our team, or what the score was'. They all laughed at the same moment, just like they were remembering together, those foolish images and memories of their younger street-playing days, the days before they had a coach and before they knew the rules of how to play well and win the game (or had these days still to arrive for some of them).

I then stated earnestly to all 5 of them; 'unfortunately, the problem that we have in the modern game, is that there are many young players out there, who either do not have a coach or do not have a good enough coach for their skill level. Or some young players, have one of those modern day player/coaches, which means their coach is still busy trying to play in their own game and not spending enough time coaching them in their game. Even worse, some young players have a really bad coach that does not have the proper qualifications or has even played the game, and therefore should not be coaching anyone else in the first instance. These unqualified, or absent or part-time coaches are ruining the game of many gifted young players. What is worse, is that the young players don't even know it yet, because they have not experienced the potential development that a great coach can add to their abilities and success and enjoyment of playing the game.

I then posed 3 questions to them:

1= 'How do you know that your coach is good enough to be giving you lessons in playing the game well?'
2=Has your coach played the game to a decent level themselves or have they achieved good results as a coach, that their advice on playing the game is actually worthy of you listening too and taking advice from?
3=Does your coach actually love and enjoy the game, so that they can then teach you how to love it and enjoy playing in it also.

Because if not, then you are likely to just love the game and play the game, to the same level that they loved it and that they have played at?

I told them honestly, that ' a big problem that you all face, is that If you only rely on your coach to tell you everything about playing your game, then what will happen to you, if the coach is not at a good enough level, or when the coach is no longer there, or if you cannot hear the coaches voice anymore, but your still on the pitch and in the middle of playing your game?'.

Therefore, in this 12-week course based on the book **The PILARS of Mind Fitness and developing a Game mindset'**, I am going to try and teach you all, how to become your 'own best coach'. So that you can love and enjoy your own game, and know what your best game is, and what your best position will be to help you win your game. Finally, being your own great coach, will help you to stop mentally, emotionally, socially and physical meandering aimlessly through your game, like you did when you were young and playing in the street without a ball or a coach.

Aldous grinned and sharply replied, 'How do we know that you are good enough to be coaching us in this', the boy was more intelligent than he realized. I laughed and said 'Your right Aldous to question me', and with a wry smile back to him I said 'hopefully one day you will learn why I am worthy of teaching you all how to improve your mind-fitness in the game'.
That day would come sooner, than we both would have imagined.

Before I gave them their second class assignment (cue the groans), then I asked them if they had ever witnessed like I had, the phenomena of when gifted sports-children had been coached for many years by their parents, but they had now reached a level that their parents coaching abilities could not develop them any further in their game. However, rather than find their children a new coach, the parents would still insist on coaching them, until finally, the children's development had become hindered enough, to stop them reaching the professional ranks. Most of them shook their head in agreement and I couldn't help but wonder if they had personal experience of this situation.

I told them that I would routinely ask young sportspeople' who was their head coach in the game'?, and when I heard the answer 'my mum and dad,' then I would ask them, 'if they thought that their mum and dad had played the game to a good enough level, in order to justify them being their head coach'?

Another question that I would pose was 'do they think that their mum and dad are happy at the level that they have achieved in the game'. Because if not, then there was a likelihood, that they could only coach children to the same level that they had achieved. If their parents had played to a high enough level, that they would be happy to reach in their game, then this was excellent. But if not, then they would need to find additional coaches, who had won the trophies and excelled at the level in the game, that they wished to win and reach.

Finally, I said to the boys, 'I firmly believe that Parents should love you more than anyone else, but that alone, does not make them a great head coach in the game'. For example, I said 'I would love playing for Manchester united, but my love of the role, isn't enough to make me any good at playing on the pitch, or to support my team-mates to score any goals, or help the team to win any games.

Class assignment 2:

In their second class assignment the boys were asked to spend 15 minutes working out, 'What does a good coach actually do for you, and why do you need a coach to help you play better?' They were to answer the following 3 questions: To aid their thinking I played them the song, 'Help' by the Beatles. I don't think it helped them though.

1=Why do I need a coach, why can't I just coach myself' or let my parents do it?
2=What can a coach actually do that will help me play better?
3=What skills makes a good coach and what traits makes a bad coach?

After 15 minutes had elapsed, then I asked them how they had got on with their assignment?

And I wrote their answers on the board in the classroom. They had done a lot better than I had expected.

Paulo mentioned, that you need a coach, to install in you '**Ambition** to want to perform well' and 'A good **Attitude** for working hard'.

I said great and wrote '**Ambition and Attitude'** on the board.

Ishmal said that he thought that a good coach '**Believed** in you and gave you **Confidence** and **Motivation** to keep going in the game, even when you were tired and wanted to give up'.

Excellent Ishmal, and I wrote, **Belief**, **Confidence** and **Motivation** on the board.

Lennon, you have been awfully quiet, so why don't you just tell us, 'why you think a good coach is useful to you'. Sheepishly, Lennon replied 'They give you 'A **Plan** and a **Strategy** for winning and scoring **Goals**, and help you deal with the frustration and depression of losing'.

Fantastic answer I yelled back, and then I proceeded to write **Plan and Strategy**, **Goals**, **Deal with loss and frustration.**

Write I said, 'next up is Aldous', he looked at me with abject boredom, as he stated, 'a coach gives you **Stress** and **fear** and makes you more **Competitive**'. They all laughed, but again were taken aback, when I said 'good answer Aldous', as many people often forget the powerful negative aspects of motivation and coaching. This seemed to silence his rebellious grin as I continued to write, **Managing stress** and **Dealing with fear** and being **Competitive**, onto the board.

Finally, I turned to Rocky, and said 'why do you think that we need a good coach and what do great Coaches do to help us play better in the game'?

Rocky, as usual had put a lot of effort into his Assignment and tried to give the best answer possible. He said, 'well Professor, I think that a coach is helpful, as they give you another objective pair of eyes to watch your performance and critically evaluate it with their experienced and knowledgeable opinion (he had obviously been reading up on this). He also said 'that a good coach gives you a greater **Awareness of your Strengths and weaknesses** in your game and improves your **Focus** on the game'. Furthermore, 'a great coach makes you **Reflect** on past performances, so that you can keep learning to make better future decisions in your game'. In addition, 'a great coach can make you more **Resilient to deal with changes** on the pitch and help you to set **personal goals'**. Rocky was not finished yet, and kept saying 'A great coach **unites the team** with a common **passion** and **purpose**, and makes you train and keep repeating your training, whilst acting as a positive **role-model** for you to become a better player in the game'. Finally, he said' a great coach can help to show you, how to spend your time and energy wisely on the pitch, so that you can last the pace for the full game'.

'Calm down Rocky', I joked as I struggled to keep up with writing his words of wisdom on the board. I hurriedly scribbled **', greater awareness, critically reflect, improve focus, better decision-making, more resilient to change, set personal goals, purpose and passion, repetition of training,** and **positive role-model',** and **how to spend your time and energy efficiently** in the game.
'A great comprehensive answer Rocky', I said 'well done'.

Between all of them, they had covered every aspect of a great coaches influence and I applauded them for it (with a hand clapping gesture).
I could see them all looking up at the board, proud yet strangely surprised at the impressive list they had created, and so they should be, as it was a fine and accurate list.

However, little did they know, as they looked up and read their own words, that they had also just created their own curriculum for the next 12 weeks.

'ambition, attitude, belief, confidence, motivation, planning, goals, deal with loss and frustration, managing stress, dealing with fear, more competitive, 'critically reflect, greater awareness, improve focus, better decision-making, more resilient to change, purpose and passion, repetition of training, positive role-model, and how to spend your time and energy wisely.

As they gazed on their list, I gave them one final question to puzzle over 'of all the traits that you have listed up here on the board, that a coach gives you for becoming greater players in the game, 'how many of them are actually related to Your physical skill and fitness levels', and how many of them are actually linked to your mental fitness or your emotional and social skills?'.

I thought I would try and use a 'journey-car-driver' analogy on them, so I said' 'Whilst we are the drivers in our life, it is important to have a good co-pilot or coach, because they can help navigate us through the most likely routes to get us where we want to be, whilst we are busy focusing on the road and trying to drive?

I told them the story of the lumberjack, who had failed to turn up for work on his first day, the other workers cursed him, but he turned every day after that for the rest of the week. At the end of the week he had chopped down more tree's, than any other lumberjack in the company. When one of them asked him where he had been on the first day he replied, 'I was at home sharpening my axe, so that I would have the sharpest axe in the company and be able to chop down more tree's than anyone else.

I looked sincerely at the boys, and said ' A good coach just helps you to sharpen your axe'.

I finished this lesson, by turning to Ishmal, and in a genuine voice, I asked him 'not to keep his focus on his father's negative, unkind and unhelpful words about what he wasn't achieving' in the game. These words from his father, were probably more about his dad's issue with how he has performed as a player and the opportunities he has wasted in his game, and not about what Ishmal has done so far with his abilities. Instead, I told Ishmal and the other boys, 'that you should always focus on what you want to achieve in the game, as this will keep your eyes on the goal and help you play better in the game'.

It was years later, that I found out, that Ishmal had been from a very early age, mentally and physically abused by his father.

Chapter 7: The Game is afoot, but do you have a Map of the journey?

PILARS Session 1: Activating Awareness versus Blissful Blindness

PILARS LAW 1= *We are an energy system and our energy flows out from our mind to our emotions and then to our behaviours and then to our social interactions and finally the energy of these social interactions flows back in again to our mind. But every action has an equal and opposite reaction, therefore the energy you give out, creates an energy back in.*

'All I have are the choices that I make and I choose to play well'.
Alan Curley

The previous first week of summer camp had been an intensive induction for the boys and the reason, that I had not given them any homework after our last session on Friday, was that I knew that they were to have their first competitive match on Sunday at the ''Summer Sports Performance Improvement Academy'. All the 5 boys in my class played for Team A at the academy, and although I didn't get to see their first match, as I was meeting an old friend In Oxford that weekend, I knew that I would always be first to see them afterwards, as I taught the Monday morning graveyard class, which followed Sunday nights big competitive game.

I genuinely found all the boys very personable and I had sincerely hoped that they would all have earned a few fantasy football league points that weekend. But like most things in life, I knew that there would be some more disappointed than others with their game performance.

I always entered the coach's staffroom, before my class (as I needed a double-caffeine shot before being bombarded by the energy of 5 teenagers). This meant, that I would always be able to see how well the boys had performed in the Sunday game from the fantasy football league chart, which was hung in pride of place in the centre of the staffroom wall. The 5 coaches had created a large poster chart for scoring the individual successes of each of the 22 players in the game. Although this was still early days in the 12 week league (week 1), I could still sense that each of the 5 coaches were very keen to see how well their own '100 million pound selection',' of 11 players were doing, as this would ultimately prove to everyone else at camp, that they knew more about the game than the other coaches did.

Here was the league results from week 1 of the fantasy football.

Week 1 Fantasy football results

Name	Value	Points this week in game	Total points from all games	Current Rating out of the 22 players
Aldous	30 mill	10	10	1*
Paulo	15 mill	9	9	4th
Rocky	10 mill	8	8	5th
Lennon	5 mill	7	7	11th
Ishmal	1 mill	6	6	14th

After I entered the class, I spent 5 minutes trying to settle the boys down from discussing their first competitive match at the summer camp. From now on, we always sat as a group in a circular fashion with no desks between us. I asked them individually to go around the circle and mention what had been the high and the low points from last week, what things had went well for them and what challenges they had faced. As you can imagine, trying to get a group of teenage boys to open up and discuss their feelings, was like trying to get Nigel Benn to hold hands with Chris Eubank.

However, I had decided to try this, because my time working in the addictions field, had taught me that good therapists are often in synchronicity with their clients, and therefore can often predict which particular challenges, victories, and disappointments, that their clients would have experienced over the previous week. They would then use these predictions to design the theme of the next session. This would help link the discussions and support offered to the client, back to the reality of their past week. This technique of being able to make the theme of each new session, relevant to the client's previous week experiences, made the sessions far more interesting and more important to the client and helped to improve their attendance at sessions. Furthermore, it served as a great convincer to the clients, that you had already visualised the different stages of their journey and therefore could help them travel further in their game next week, in order to help them reach their next desired destination.

The boys were still buzzing from the fact that their team (Team A), had won the first game of the first week and Aldous was sitting particularly peacock-like, as he had scored a hat-trick and was top of the league with 10 points. I noticed how engaged they all had been when discussing the fantasy football league scores awarded to themselves and others and so, as a bit of a joke, I said to them, 'that I was going to start my own fantasy class league table with them, regarding how well they were performing in my class and with their homework'. To my surprise, they all thought that this was a good idea, which I should have suspected, since I was dealing with 5 young competitive sportsman.

So, I quickly devised a class poster and put their names on it. I copied the format of the fantasy football league poster from the coaches staffroom, which had columns for their potential future value, followed by the points scored that week in the game, followed by the total points scored to date at summer camp, followed by their relative rating to the other 22 young players at summer sports academy.

Once, we had finished creating the fantasy classroom league table then I hung it up on the wall and I awarded all of them points based, on their performance in class last week.

After they had settled down AGAIN, from the excitement (for some) or the disappointment (for others), of seeing their class fantasy league scores, then I got them all to repeat looking up at the list that they had jointly compiled in the previous class assignment called, 'What does a good coach actually do for you, and why do you need a coach to help you play better?'
The list that they had created highlighted the main areas, 'That a great coach helps us develop, so that we can perform better in the game'.

'Ambition, Attitude, Awareness, Belief, Competitiveness, Confidence, Decision-making, Improve Focus, Motivation, Planning, Goals, Deal with Fear, Loss and Frustration, Purpose and Passion, critical Reflection, Repetition of training, Role-models, Resilience and Managing Stress.

I repeated to them, that I agreed with their list and then proceeded to mention, 'That today, we will be starting the first of our 12 session certificate program called **'The PILARS of Mind Fitness and developing a Game mindset'**, or that I have cleverly shortened to **'So you think you could be a coach?"**.

'This course will help you all gain a certificate in becoming your 'very own great personal coach' and will support you to develop your players full potential, by increasing your mind fitness levels and finding your most useful game-mindset. Both of these will allow your player to have the most enjoyable and successful playing career as possible.

In each weekly coaching session, we will look at 5 components of the skill that needs nurtured in your player, in order for them to improve their game. I then told them that because the 1st PILARS law states' every action has an equal and opposite reaction'. Which we know courtesy of Newton, then each skill that we will discuss, will have its equivalent trait on the opposite end of the spectrum. These are linked to each other and influence each other. If one gains a level, then the other loses a level. For example; confidence and anxiety are linked at opposite ends of the same spectrum.

I proceeded to write these up on the class board.

1=What is the definition of the skill that we are talking about, and what is its opposing skill?
2=Why is the skill important in helping our players game performance?
3=Where does the skill come from?
4=How do we measure or assess if our player has the correct amount of this skill ?
5=What techniques can we teach our players, so that they can change their level of this skill?

When I turned back round to face the boys, then I noticed that Ishmal and lennon were shuffling a piece of paper between them and the source of the paper was causing them to get all animated in that annoyingly energetic way that only teenagers can do!
I initially thought it was some secret love-letter but to my disappointment, when I yelled for them to calm down and try and explain to me what all the fuss was about, then they told me that 'Frank the head coach had a tradition, wherein at the start of each Summer camp he buried a treasure-box with £10,000 somewhere in the vast grounds of the camp. Frank had released the one and only clue this morning to the whereabouts of the box and the first boy that found it would get to keep the £10,000.
It was obvious by the excitement with which these boys were ogling over the clue, that they valued money over love-letters.
The clue that frank had given each boy read like this,
'The sooner that you can see the process, then the next part of the journey will unveil itself and the treasure will be found'.

When they had each eventually finished reading the clue out loud, and looked back at me, they all seemed to notice that I had a strange grin on my face. I proceeded to ask them, whether they thought that it was a coincidence, but today's first 'mind fitness and game-mindset' coaching session', would be to create a 'Skill-Awareness Map' of the improvement journey which they wanted to travel on and arrive at, by the end of the 12 week summer camp.

Unfortunately, my wonderful power of analogy was completely lost on them.

I then proceeded to show them the first of my class Powerpoint slides (to which they all simultaneously groaned in agony). I had decided to start the class with a slide image of the London underground map, because I wanted them to realise that trying to make a change and improve their own game, (just like life) was just like going on a journey.

I then asked them, 'if you were wanting to improve and travel further in your game, then what is the first question you would need to ask yourself before going on this change improvement journey'?

Ishmal replied 'Where you currently are'? Excellent I said, 'you need an **awareness** of where you currently are'.

Then once you know where you are, then what do you need to ask yourself next?

'Where you want to go, sir', and before they all laughed at him again, I said 'excellent Ishmal'. He seemed to be enjoying this lesson.

'Only, when you have an **awareness** of where you are, then can you work out your **ambition** of where you would like to go to next'. We call this your new **desired destination**.

Don't worry I said boys, because we will cover '**Ambition'**, in our next class.

But in this class, we are focusing on the first step of the journey, which is the **awareness** of where you have been, and where you currently are.

I then asked them, 'if we have an **awareness** of where we are and we also have the **ambition** to want to move forward to somewhere else, then what would you need, to help you get to this new **desired destination**'? Aldous laughed and quickly answered 'Google maps?'. 'Amazing', Aldous I exclaimed, 'yes, we need a map to show us the best or easiest way for us to get from where we are, to where we want to be'. Aldous looked disappointed that his answer was actually correct.

Then I proceeded to ask them, 'Why is it on google maps, that we still need to enable our location and input where we are just now and where we want to get too'?

Rocky quickly replied, 'so that you can figure out the distance between these locations and how long that it will take you to get there'. 'Yes, you are right Rocky', I grinned, 'you can't get to where you want to be, if you don't know where you are just now and how far apart these places are from one another'. You need this information, in order to work out how long you will have to travel for, before you can expect to arrive at where you want to be instead, your **desired destination**.

Lennon quickly joked 'Yes, professor, you also need to know how much the ticket will cost to get you there, because if you haven't got the money, then you will be kicked off the train before arriving (they all laughed, letting me know that Lennon had obviously been caught jumping train fares before).

'You are more correct than you think Lennon', I shouted back at him amidst the laughter (once again he also looked disappointed at getting the answer right). You also need an awareness of how much this journey is going to cost you and if you have the enough for the journey.

I then asked them, 'if they knew what the specific map on my powerpoint slide was?'

Paulo said it was the London underground map (as him and Lennon had visited there last month).

'That's correct Paulo', I said, 'but can you tell me why I decided to use this particular map, when I could have shown you any map?'

he replied ' is it because there are many zones in London, and if you haven't paid the fare for the correct ticket then you cannot proceed through all the zones' (once again they all looked at Lennon and laughed).

'No I said', to his dismay, but I did like his answer, And thought that I may add this in to my future lecture material.

'I don't know and don't care much for London', Aldous shrugged, but rocky in a lightbulb moment said, 'Professor, is it because there are many different routes on the map that you can take to get where you want to be'. 'Excellent rocky' I said, 'Yes, the London underground was designed, so that if one line was closed, then you could still always get to where you wanted to be, by making a change onto another route instead'.

I said 'the complex London underground, is just like life boys, if you do not have a good map, which accurately shows you where you are and the quickest easiest routes for getting to where you want to be, then you have little or no chance of getting there'. Furthermore, 'if one route on your journey gets closed, then you need a decent map, which can show you, where you can make the changes, so as to keep you moving forward towards your **desired destination'.**

I looked up expecting a round of clever applause, but instead they all just stared blankly back at me, these boys just never seemed to appreciate my amazing analogies.

By now, I was on a roll with the journey analogies and so I told them that, 'for most journeys, once you know where you currently are and where you want to be instead, then you would next need to work out the distance, time, effort and cost required to make that journey successful'. If you are not willing to travel for that length of time, or if you are not willing to pay the cost of the fare (I stared over at Lennon), then the chances are, you will not be able to successfully reach your **desired destination.**

Technique 1: Activating your Awareness

They were not happy to hear that they now had a 10 minute class assignment. This involved them creating their own 'game improvement map'. This exercise consisted of the boys deciding one improvement to their game which they hoped to have achieved by the end of the 12 week camp (their desired destination). In order to help them create their map, I played them the song 'Bless the Broken road' by Rascal Flatts. The music did not seem to help their creative juices flow.

This is what they told me:

-Paulo said, 'he would like to get **more confident to push himself forward** in the game'.

- Ishmal, 'wanted to improve **his focus and resilience** as he felt he gets **worried and distracted** when a game gets tough and then he **gives up too easily'.**

-Lennon, stated that he 'wants to work on his **discipline** on the pitch, as he felt that sometimes when a decision goes against him, then he gets **frustrated and stressed** and gets sent off after **losing his temper'.**

-Aldous shrugged his shoulders and grunted, **'To be better than everyone else on the pitch'** (he was always about the glory and never about the enjoyment of playing in a team game)

-Rocky pondered for a while and then said 'he felt he could **score more goals** by improving **his awareness of the game and his decision-making abilities** in front of goal'.

I thanked them all for their honest answers, and I wrote down each of their names next to what they wanted to have achieved by the end of the 12 week camp (their desired destination).

I then stuck their names and desired destinations onto the large poster of the London underground map, which I had hung up in the classroom wall, next to their fantasy class league table.

Next, I asked them all 'to assess how far away they currently thought that they were, from being able to achieve their desired destination by the end of summer camp.

A score of 10, was the equivalent of thinking you would never reach it, as it was too far away and a score of 1 was the equivalent of thinking you were almost there already.

These were their scores, of how far away they considered themselves to be at this point

-Paulo= 9   (he really did lack confidence in himself)

-Ishmal= 9   (he really did get anxious and over-worry about everything)

-Lennon=10   (he clearly thought that you could never learn to train your emotions)

-Aldous= 1   (he did not suffer from any self-confidence issues)

-Rocky= 5   (his awareness on making good decisions was clearly improving already)

I, physically applauded them on their honest if not deluded assessments (whilst casting a frown over at Aldous).

I told them, that they had now completed stage 1 of the 'Change-Game', which was called

'Activating awareness versus blissful blindness'.

I told them that 'In this initial stage of change, then your awareness battles with your blindness. If you can activate your awareness' then you win the knowledge of where you currently are (reality), and how far away this is from where you would like to be (desired destination). I mentioned that 'Activating your awareness levels' was like being captivated by a new form of light which someone has switched on and it now casts an altered view of your environment into your eyes, which makes you now see things differently for the first time and want to be somewhere else. Its opposing trait blindness, is when you are not looking at yourself and your life and asking the question 'are you happy with who you are and where you are? But rather are just blindly meandering and allowing life to take you where it wants, with no particular destination in mind. I told them my adaptation of John Lennon's quote 'life is what will happen to you, unless you get busy making other plans'. They were not impressed.

Moving forward in our life Journey?

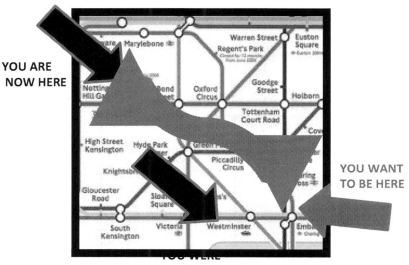

YOU ARE
NOW HERE

YOU WANT
TO BE HERE

YOU WERE
HERE

then got them to watch 1 video which highlighted that we are all in an unequal game, then another video which was linked to testing their awareness levels and the third video was the Shawshank redemption parole scene, where they got to practice talking to their past selves and future selves and what they would like to say to them. After they had finished talking to their past and future selves, then I gave them all a 'Mindfulness mask' and I asked them to put it on and close their eyes and now become more aware of their breathing. Then I asked them just to imagine just one thing that they were currently grateful for that they had in their present life. This was the 5 boys first introduction to **mindfulness.**

When they opened their eyes, then I said to them that it often amazed me, 'how many people spent more time looking at where they wanted to go on 'google-maps on their phone', and not enough time thinking about where they wanted to travel to next on their 'life-maps'.
It also seemed like it is more important for people to ensure that they have their 'current location' enabled on their mobile phone, yet they do not spend any time on assessing their awareness of where they are currently located in their life, and if they are happy with this location' or would prefer to move on to another **desired destination.**

To summarise this session, I said 'that every journey starts with you Activating your awareness, and this is the equivalent of suddenly switching on the 'location enabled' function on your phone and realizing that you would like to make a change to your current life-location. Because, now that you know where you are located on your life-map, then this will help you to work out how far away you are from where you want to be, your next desired destination.
However, your next desired destination is linked to the concept of 'Ambition', and I joked to them that 'do not worry about this as we will be discussing ambition in the next class', (and I could tell from their apathy, that they just couldn't wait).

Then they asked me to total up their scores awarded from todays class and create the class league table next to their football league table, both of which were hung on the wall next to their London Underground 'Game-improvement map'.

This was the point results from week 1 of the fantasy football/class league table.
As they could see their class results did not mirror their football results, but I jovially said to them **' don't worry lads, as there is a still plenty of time left for you to play in the game yet, and who says I am talking about football?'**, but they did not appreciate my jovial tones.

Finally, as the bell went and they were all scurrying out of the room 'I uttered the phrase that they would quickly come to despise

Remember boys, I said, 'You never lose in this game, you only win or you learn'.

Week 1 Fantasy football results

Name	Value	Points this week in game	Total points from all games	Current Rating out of the 22 players
Aldous	30 mill	10	10	1st
Paulo	15 mill	9	9	4th
Rocky	10 mill	8	8	5th
Lennon	5 mill	7	7	11th
Ishmal	1 mill	6	6	14th

Week 1 Fantasy class results

Name	Value	Points this week in class	Total points from all classes	Current Rating out of the 5 in class
Rocky	10 mill	9	9	1st
Paulo	15 mill	7	7	2nd
Ishmal	1 mill	6	6	3rd
Lennon	5 mill	4	4	4th
Aldous	30 mill	3	3	5th

Chapter 8: Where is your desired destination?

PILAR Session 2: Accelerating Ambition versus Anchoring Acceptance

PILARS LAW 2= *'Energy can neither be created nor destroyed just converted from one form to another'. We are all born with potential energy and the purpose of the game, is to spend or convert this potential energy over your lifetime, with the aim of scoring as many enjoyable, proud, happy and pleasurable experiences and success goals as possible, or to avoid as many painful, uncomfortable or embarrassing experiences as possible. One final aim of the game, is to convert our potential energy into creating a memory and story of our game, that will remain and live on for people to talk about, long after our game has ended.*

'A person's worth is no greater than the worth of their ambitions'.
Marcus Aurelius Antoninus

When the '5 special boys' (their phrase not mine) returned for their next class, I noticed that they were all sitting in the circular array of chairs, but that everyone was doing that thing where they either were looking down at the floor or up at ceiling (rather than make eye contact with the coach or anyone else). So, I halted the silence with asking them if anyone had found the £10,000 treasure-box yet? By figuring out the Phrase: **'The sooner that you can see the process, then the next part of the journey will unveil itself and the treasure will be found'.**

They all groaned 'no', so I then asked them 'How did your game go yesterday?'
They all answered in derisory unison 'we drew 2-2', and were not happy campers, when I said 'that's not too bad is it?"

Rocky said, 'we should have won as we were 2-0 up at half-time, but the coach told us to sit back in the second half and defend our advantage, but we lost 2 goals in the last 20 minutes'.

That's tough I said, 'what would you do differently now' if you were back in that past situation again, but now with your future knowledge. Aldous quickly mentioned 'that he would sack the coach and get another one'. I could see that Aldous was getting annoyed and he was getting more animated as he recalled the poor strategy decision by the coach, which they were forced to follow against their own better judgement and which had cost them the game. I sensed that this incident had been one of many frustrations for him, with regards someone else making decisions on his part without asking him his opinion, and those decisions, ultimately costing him dearly. Aldous continued in his rant; 'saying that he wished he had a coach 'who would have more faith and more ambition to want to score more goals, and the vision to see that to keep moving forward, was the way to win this game'.

I always remember thinking at that moment, that Aldous subconsciously knew a lot more than he consciously realized, but that his inability to critically reflect on himself and his life and learn from it, would cost him dearly in the game. I told them' That I did understand their anger and frustration and that I had sympathy for them because at their age, they still have to take instructions from loads of coaches and often get told what to do in their own game, without having much of a voice to state their own preferred game strategies. What is even more frustrating for them, is that sometimes they have to follow coaches who get it wrong or actually know less than them or even worse, coaches who have played the game less well, than they will in the future.

I told them all not to worry about their scores as it was still early days in the game.
This was their second session of the Mind Fitness certificate course that I had designed, called, **'So you think you could be a coach?"**. 'The course would help them gain a certificate in becoming their very own great personal coach and develop their mind fitness and their game-mindset and therefore become their best game-player possible (I could see that they were not convinced of my sales-pitch).

So, I repeated to them 'that each week, we will look at 5 components of the skill that needs nurtured in your player, in order for them to improve their game.
I proceeded to write these up on the class board.

1=What is the definition of the skill that we are talking about and what is its opposing skill?
2=Why is it important in helping our players game performance?
3=Where does the skill come from?
4=How do we measure or assess, if our player has the correct amount of this skill?
5=What techniques can we teach our players, so that they can change their level of this skill?

In this session I said, 'we will be learning how to **'Improve the ambition of your player'.**
Instantly, I heard the usual teenage grunt response, obviously this statement had went down like a dodgy striker in the penalty box.
Interestingly, I said to them, 'that you all had thought that your coach was not ambitious enough this week and that is why you lost the game'. 'Well, maybe you are right, a coach who lacks

ambition will not be able to install ambition in their players and this may cost them all dearly in the game', as no one in the team, will think they are worthy enough, to try and move forward in their game and travel further to other desired destinations'.

So I repeated again, hoping for a more energetic response this time, this week in our course **'so you think you could be a coach'**, then we will be learning how to increase your players ambition and the quality of the Goals they wish to score in the game.

Aldous confidently voiced back, 'that it was not possible for his goals to get anymore higher quality than they were already'.

Sadly for him, time would tell a different story.

1= Definition of Ambition and Acceptance.

I asked the boys if they had ever heard those familiar phrases; 'You have no ambition, or you need to have more ambition, or 'why don't you set yourself some goals and you will succeed'. but in this class, we are going to look at what does 'ambition' actually mean and what are goals?

As a mind fitness coach the definition you will learn in this class is that by a players 'Ambition' and its opposite skill 'Acceptance', then these will be defined as, (and I wrote these definitions up on the wall):

Ambition= The desire to want to add more into your future than you currently have in the present.

Acceptance = To be satisfied with what you have in the present and to not seek or desire anymore.

2=Why is Ambition, important in helping your players game performance.

So, In our inner circle of discussion, I asked them all the question, 'Why do you think as a coach, that helping your player to amplify their ambition, will help them in their game performances and professional career'?

Paulo said= 'So that they want to keep learning and getting better at the game'.
Ishmal= 'So that they can remember what they said they would achieve, and then look back with happiness and pride when they achieve it'.
Lennon= 'So that they know, what is important to focus on'.
Aldous, (as cool as ever)= 'So that they know what they are worth, and can keep earning more money to spend on more stuff'.
Rocky='So that they always have something else to keep striving and aiming for in the game, no matter how long they have been playing for, or what they have already achieved'
(This boy was good).

'Top answers', I replied. Yes, the more ambition that your player has, will help to keep driving them on to develop their game further, no matter how good they are at the moment. Ambition also helps a player to enjoy their past achievements which makes them happy and proud, and which stops them getting complacent and lowering their rate of development. Furthermore, ambition helps a player to increase their confidence with every victory they achieve, which in turn, increases their sense of self-worth and value. Finally, no matter what stage of the game or what level they are currently playing at, then ambition always gives them something personal to aim for achieving, even in a team game, in order to taste the sweet victory of success as an individual, as well as within a team.

In summary, I said to the boys 'having ambition helps to give your player, Past proud glories to enjoy reminiscing about, current focus on continued improvement, increased self-worth and confidence, and future feelings of individual and team success'. 'Not a bad lot', I said, when you consider how easy ambition is to get.

I then pointed to the London Undergound 'Change-map' on the wall, which we had previously used in the first 'activating awareness' session and where each of the 5 boys had placed where they currently were in the game and where they wanted to be at the end of the summer camp. I told them that Ambition on your map, is the equivalent of having new **desired destinations,** which you wish to move forward to and reach in the game. Whereas acceptance, was being happy and comfortable staying where you currently are on the map.

Thus, **Ambition, accelerates** you forward in the game and **acceptance, anchors** you to where you are?

Therefore, a player in your team who lacks ambition will have not much desire to try and improve his game for the future, and as a coach this can be a problem for your team.

3=Where does our ambition levels come from?

So, In our circle of trust, I next asked them 'if we understand why 'ambition' is important to helping your player perform better in the game, then 'where do you get your ambition levels from'?

Paulo said= 'You get them from your coach' (he obviously thought, that this was the answer I was hoping to hear every time)

Ishmal= 'You get them from watching your idols, who you wish to play like'.

Lennon= 'You get them from your beliefs and values', (budding psychologist)

Aldous= Proclaimed with a bitter tone, 'You get them from your parents, as they are always nagging you to have more ambition'.

I replied, 'Unfortunately, Aldous once again you are more correct than you think, many of us do get our ambition levels from our parents, as they often try and influence us to fulfill their past failed goals and ambitions'. This reminded me of a great scene from only fools and horses, where del-boy whilst holding his new born son in his arms in the hospital, tells him that this time next year his son will be a millionaire' and will be able to tell him all about how good it felt., as he never managed it.

Rocky='Professor, you get them from using your mind to visualise and project the future you would like to have, and then you work backwards in time, to devise a Plan and strategy for the smaller steps that you would need to achieve along that journey'.

(I was now thinking of offering this boy a job in my mind fitness and life improvement centre).

'Tremendous', I said 'once again all your answers fit the question'.

Your ambition levels can be gained from many different influences or sources. These include from coaches who give you vision and strategies, from your playing idols who give you a model for which to admire and copy. From your own personal values and beliefs about what success is and what type of success you would like to have in your game.

You also get ambition from your parents, who make you work harder and study, because they see this as a good foundation for your future. Whilst, you are convinced that their only goal in life, is too stop you from enjoying the pleasure of the present-life. And Finally, yes you get it from your own mind and what information it has processed about what it thinks you are worth, and what you hope to deserve and experience in your future.

So as a coach, the important thing to remember about your players ambition level, is that the more you can give them a sense of self-worth and discuss what possibilities are out there using examples of other people's achievements, then the more they will believe that they can reach these **desired destinations.** This in turn, will help them to work harder and be more committed, to spending their current Skill, Energy and Time in the game (their game-SET), into converting their ambitions into real-life results.

This is why on your map, it is always worth having other people on it, like role models who have reached these **desired destinations** as they can inspire you forward.

Lennon suddenly asked, 'but what if in your life, you have never really known anyone that has moved forward sir',

I smiled and answered 'sadly, you raise a very good point Lennon', 'in life, it is a lot harder for people to improve and develop, if the environment that they have grown up in, has never really shown them anyone who has achieved moving forwards'.

This truth would become more real for Lennon, than he would ever know at this point.

To prove this point, I told them a story about a growing branch of psychology called 'successology'. I had been one of the pioneers of this movement years ago when I first started working with professional sportspeople. It basically studied successful people in all different Walks of life i.e. business, science, Arts, media, and Sports. Its aim was to work out which were the traits or skills that all successful people had in common, and this would then act as a map to help others know what to do or nurture, in order to become more successful.

I was particularly interested in studying the parenting of the successful people who came from poor, disadvantaged, less-educated and addiction-riddled backgrounds. These individuals were of interest, because they had defied the odds and not followed in those environmental and social footsteps of their families, friends and peers. My conclusions were; that one of the biggest common denominators linking these successful people, was that their parents (or other role-models) had helped to develop great levels of ambition within them, by telling them they were better than their environment and could become whatever they wanted. In addition, their parents (or other role-models), had helped nurture ambition and goal-setting in them, usually by telling them stories and examples about other people's glories and success. It was these stories which I found particularly interesting, as it was their recall of them that seemed to be the most influential aspect of what made them ambitious and able to set up their own powerful future goals, from a very early age, despite the people and the environment that surrounded them.

Every one of these successful individuals had then went on to successfully achieve their 'goals against the odds', which was especially impressive given the early environments that they had been exposed to.

I guess that once they had the desire of ambition and a powerful vision of their future goals (desired destinations), then they must have committed to spend their Skill, Energy and Time very wisely in the game, in order to achieve their level of success.

I told the boys that Mary Ainsworth had shown many years ago, that Positive Stories from parents to children are such a great way of building positive secure attachments.

Therefore, it always made me wonder, 'if we know that this story technique is so powerful in nurturing ambition and goals, in order to help gain more future happiness and success'. Then why do so many parents and coaches never seem to tell nurturing stories to their children about success or help the young players practice visualising seeing themselves reaching their future **desired destinations with examples of others.**

Maybe the honest answer was that these coaches, did not have coaches who gave them stories of ambition, and so they too just accepted, that where they were, was good enough or that they couldn't travel any further anyway?

4=How do we know if our player has the correct level of ambition before each game?

So as a coach, 'the important thing to remember about your players ambition, is that the more ambition they have, then the harder they will physically sweat and work to keep moving forward in their game and the more committed they will be to spending their Skill, Energy and Time in the game (game-SET), in order to convert these, into goals and positive results for the team.

So, my next question to all of them became '**As coach, how will you assess, if your player has the correct level of ambition before each game'?**

Here were there answers:
Paulo said= 'You get it from the effort they have put into training that week'. (again, he obviously had been talking to coaches)
Ishmal= 'You ask them what they think the result is going to be'?
Lennon= 'You get it from their confidence in the dressing room'.
Aldous= 'You get it from asking them 'how many goals they are going to score, and how they will celebrate each goal'?
Rocky='Professor, you ask them about what they see happening in the game and how well they think they will perform'.

Great, I said 'once again collectively, you are all correct in that these are all ways to measure someone's levels of ambition before a game'.
You get it from the physical effort that they have put into the training before the game. You get it from the amount of time that they have spent on imagining the future game and the future scoreline. You get it from their confidence about how well they think they will perform.

You get it from the specific level of detail that they can describe about how they are planning on playing. Finally, you can assess their ambition levels based on how well they have visualised all the enjoyment in celebrating the victory afterwards, as this will help them to keep spending their Skill, Energy and Time until the game has ended, as their minds will be convinced that it will be worth it.

I finished by asking them, 'who was their favourite players and teams in the game'. Was it not, those that always kept going and kept fighting in the game right up until the whistle blew, and often got a great result against the odds. Whereas In contrast, was it not frustrating watching players and teams who often just accepted defeat and stopped competitively playing, long before their time had even ended in the game.

I told the boys that research has shown, that you are 4 times more likely to score a goal if you have one in mind. Yet, most young players, if you ask them what their future goal is for the Skill, Energy and Time that they are currently spending in the game, then they often don't have one?

5= What techniques can we use, to help to change our players level of ambition (increase it or decrease it).

So in our last section we worked out as a coach, '**how to measure if our player has the correct level of ambition before each game**'?

So my next question to all of the boys became, '**As coach, if you have worked out that your player does not have the correct level of ambition you require for the game, then how can you help them improve it before the game starts**'?

I then proceeded to show the boys a technique for gaining more ambition by creating **SWEATY** Goals that will keep driving you forward towards your **ambitions or desired destinations.**

Successful players, realise that how well they perform in each and every new game from now on, will play a small but important step in moving them forward on the map towards their future desired destinations.

I then told them the story of Roger Bannister (the first man to break the 4 minute mile). This achievement had actually been considered impossible by many experts, but one day Roger Bannister, worked out that if he broke the 1 mile race into smaller units and had a pacer who could run at a certain speed for each of these smaller units, then as long as he could keep up with each of these pacers, then by the end of the race he himself would have ran the complete mile in under 4 minutes.

He achieved this and proved the value of breaking any ambition down into smaller goals. Incidentally, I told the boys that within 1 year of Roger Bannister achieving this previously considered impossible task. Then hundreds of people had now also achieved the 4 minute mile (which further proved the power of 'belief 'in helping people to achieve their goals). Once these others knew it could be done, then they now believed that they could do it also and tried harder. This highlights the power of role-models and examples for inspiring people to believe they can achieve more also.

I said to them' that you have all heard the phrase 'You need to focus more on your goals' but what does this actually mean?

Therefore, as a mind fitness coach the definition you will learn in this class is that by a player's 'Goals' and its opposite skill 'fears', are defined as

Goals= 'What you hope to have gained, achieved or experienced in the future.

Fears= 'What you do not hope to have gained, achieved or experienced in the future.

So you can see boys that so far we have covered;
-Ambition is wanting to become better and gain more in the future
-Goals are those specific things in the future which you want to have scored or gained from your Skill, Energy and Time that you have spent In the game (game-SET).

I then pointed back up at the London Underground Map on the wall, on which their 5 names were highlighted from our awareness session, which placed them where they currently are, and then from our ambition session which placed them where they would like to be (their desired destination).
Goals I proceeded to tell them are those smaller stepping stones, pit-stops and places along the way that you have to reach first on the map, before you can finally get to your ambition or desired destination.
I told the boys, that there is an old saying in psychology, 'if the mind can see it, then it will believe it, and when it believes it, then it is more likely to achieve it'.
I told them that I would show them how to create the best goals possible, which I had termed **'SWEATY'** goals as they make your mind vividly see them, which helps it to become more motivated and able to convince our bodies to work physically harder and SWEAT to achieve them.

Moving forward in our life Journey?

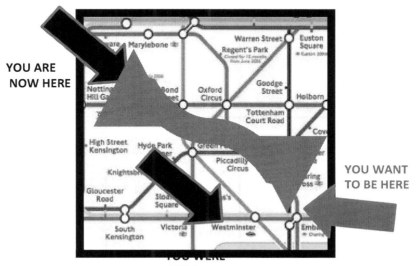

**YOU ARE
NOW HERE**

**YOU WANT
TO BE HERE**

HERE

SWEATY GOALS

So I now taught them the technique of setting SWEATY-goals. These are Goals which your mind has constructed so vividly, that you can visualize them clearly, and imagine their benefits, just like they are real future scenes in the film of your life. Usually, it means that you are able to describe your SWEATY goal to others, so that they can imagine it clearly also.

The reason it works, is that our motivation levels are initially generated in our mind, so only when your players mind can truly imagine a SWEATY goal and believes that it can be real, will it then decide that it now wants it enough, to begin to motivate the body into action. Results and changes are gained only from sweating and working harder to make them happen (SWEATY Goals).

I told the young players, that I had first created SWEATY goals when working with a female hockey player, who was having trouble getting motivated for training sessions. However, although I had created SWEATY goals specifically for sportspeople, I had found that they worked well for everyone who had an **ambition to change** and reach a new **desirable destination.**

Whether it was beating an opponent or beating an addiction or beating the mediocrity of their life, then creating SWEATY goals will make it easier and quicker to hit your target. I had found that they worked better than traditional SMART goals, especially with Sportsman as SMART goals were realistic and thus did not trigger the same level of ambition and therefore do not generate the same level of motivation, which is required if an idea has to generate SWEAT and action in order to turn into a real-life result.

I told the boys that 'The important thing to remember about goals is 'that they are just future ideas, images and scenes which your mind creates and projects for you'. Your mind acts just like a projector by focusing images and scenes, so that you can visualize them, like they are appearing in front of you. But your SWEATY Goal projections are only useful, if you keep focused on them, and the picture looks clear and vivid enough to view them, and the goals that you are watching are stimulating and motivating enough, to make you want to SWEAT your focus, energy, skill and time into making the present projections become a future reality.

Research has shown that the clearer the goal, that the mind can create and focus on, then the more stimulated it becomes to want to experience that goal. The more the mind wants it, then the more of your energy, skill and time, it will allow your player to focus and spend on achieving it. Remember, that to achieve most goals, then you need your players mind to help them focus and spend and convert more of their skill, energy and time into whatever is required to gain that goal . That is why SWEATY goals have been shown to be the best, as they help create the most vivid images in your brain to give it maximal motivation. If your goals are 'SWEATY', then your brain will be able to see clearly now, how great your future can be when you achieve it, and so it will start to help coach you, to make you sweat and work harder to achieve the SWEATY goal.

There is a quote that sums this up, 'Once the mind can conceive it enough, to see and believe it, then it will help motivate the body to achieve it'.

I tried to highlight the power of goal-setting by telling the boys the story of the Olympic gold decathlete who when interviewed, would often say that he performed and won exactly like he had already seen happening in his mind before the tournament began. He was a natural winner and goal-visualizer.

I then laughed and quipped, He may have been a decathlete, but he was also great at scoring GOALS, (whilst throwing my foot out and proudly saying) –'back of the net'.

My sporting humour was lost on these boys.

I, then told the young players that I would now teach them my secret formula for creating SWEATY goals.

The following was my secret formula for creating SWEATY goals

S= Stands for SPECIFIC

Firstly boys I said, 'The 'S' in 'SWEATY goals, stands for 'Specific'.

Your SWEATY GOALS have to have be written with specific details that you can measure if you have achieved it or not, therefore it needs to have a number attached to the goal.

For example, saying that you want ' to lose weight' would not fit as a SWEATY goal as it is not specific enough, but saying I want to lose 5kg or get down to a size 10 in a dress, would be more specific.

The more specific the goal is, the more the brain can measure and see what it has to achieve, and the clearer the mind can see it, then the more stimulated it becomes to allow you to focus your time and energy on getting it. This is why all sporting competitions use numbers as a way of measuring who has won. It is also why professional sportspeople measure their stats and personal best performances, because they want numbers to focus on, as these will keep motivating them to try and improve their games performance.

W= Stands for 'WANT & WHY'

The 'W' In SWEATY I said to the boys stands for 'Want and Why".

As it is Important that 'SWEATY goals have to have be written in the positive, therefore they must be about things that YOU WANT to have , happen, gain or experience, rather than things that you don't want to experience (as these are actually your fears and Anxieties and you don't want to be making a list and focusing on these)'.

This is because, your mind generates the feelings within you, based on what you are focusing on. Therefore if you focus its time and energy on something positive that you want, then it starts to get motivated and think more about having them (which is good and helpful for your confidence) as you will get more attracted to spending more of your Skill, energy and time on achieving them. However, if you focus your mind on something you don't want (a Fear), then it will begin to generate feelings of stress and anxiety within you (which is less helpful to you, when thinking of achieving your goals). In terms of your improvement- map, then focusing your mind on goals is the equivalent of looking at the different routes which will get you to the places that you want to visit. Focusing on fears is like working out how to get to places that you don't want to visit anyway.

To highlight this, I told them the story of the Irish Boxer I had worked with, he was having trouble with issues of stress and anxiety leading up to the 'big-fight', and these were stopping him from sleeping and eating properly, as well as affecting his mental and physical energy levels. So when I asked him what his goals were for the boxing match, this is what he answered; 'well I definitely don't want to get knocked out In the first round, and I don't want all my fans to see a boring fight and I just don't won't to let people down by not boxing well and embarrass myself by not winning'. It had dawned on me why he was anxious and worried and was having sleepless nights, he was too busy thinking about what he didn't want to happen in his game (his FEARS), rather than focusing on what he did want to happen in his game (his SWEATY GOALS). I told them that FEARS and GOALS are just opposite ends of the same spectrum of future-thinking. It is like the law of Physics that states, **'EVERY ACTION HAS AN EQUAL AND OPPOSITE REACTION'.** People often make the mistake of thinking that when they are focusing on their negative fears, that they are actually thinking about their positive goals, and so they get the opposite feelings that they hoped for. I guess this is a common mistake many people make, who suffer from stress and anxiety in their game.

I always imagine SWEATY GOALS, to be just like a future shopping list of things you want to have and add to your trolley. So, **you would never go shopping with a list of things that you didn't want, because if you did, then you would leave the shop without the things you had hoped to get , because you were too busy focused on things you didn't want or need.**

I next mentioned to the boys that 'The other important aspect of SWEATY GOALS, is knowing why you want each GOAL and convincing your mind how much that it will be worth SWEATING for, in order to achieve it and experience the benefits that it will being to you and your life.

This is required because travelling to each next SWEATY GOAL (next desired destination) on your map, takes more skill, energy and time, than staying where you are on the map. Your mind needs convinced about why it should allow you to spend more of your focus, energy, skill and time on moving forward to achieve this SWEATY GOAL. Therefore, you always need to convince your mind, that achieving the SWEATY GOAL will add value, happiness or success to you or your future life. If not, then it will not stay focused enough on giving you the energy, time and motivation, which is required to keep you moving forwards to your **SWEATY GOAL (next desired destination).**

E= Stands for EXAMPLE.

Boys I said, 'The 'E' in SWEATY stands for 'example'. SWEATY goals have to be able to give your mind an EXAMPLE of the GOAL being achieved before (either by yourself or someone else).

Your mind will allow you to spend more of your focus, energy skill and time on achieving a goal, which it is already convinced can be done (hence why we need an example) and that it perceives this new destination as better than where you currently are on the map. The best convincer to the mind, is often to give it an example of you or someone else, having achieved the goal before. Remember, If the mind has seen it, then it believes it, and this will help it to motivate you more to achieve it'. This is the equivalent on the map to you or someone else, already having visited the desired destination and enjoyed being in that place a lot more than where you currently are. Remember the Roger Bannister story of the 4 minute mile, or the successful people who had been told about examples when they were young of people like them doing wonderful things, which had then inspired them to go and do the same.

A= Stands for AMBITION

Next Boys I mentioned 'The 'A' in SWEATY goals have to lead to one of your current life's AMBITION. Unlike SMART goals which are realistic, then SWEATY goals are about stimulating your mind to fire you up for motivation, your mind does not get very motivated by achieving 'reality'. However, it does get more stimulated by focusing on thoughts and images of gaining ambitions and exciting results from the skill, energy and time that you will need it, to allow you to spend, before you can achieve the SWEATY GOAL. Thinking of SWEATY goals which leads to our ambitions, motivates our minds more, and this is why they make us willing to get SWEATY and work harder, so that we can turn them into real-life results and move us to our next **desired destination.**

T= Stands for TIME (Start and Finish time).
'Boys, the 'T' IN SWEATY goals I said 'stands for TIME a "Start and Finish TIME.
There is a quote that states **'The longer something takes to happen, the less likely it will happen'.** So, just like any sporting race or game, then a SWEATY goal has to have a start-time (when you will begin the process of improvement or change) and an end-time placed upon it (when you expect to have reached the desired destination).
This helps to stop us procrastinating about it, because we now have a Start-time to create a travel-plan and set it into action. The Finish-time is useful for us, as it helps to remind us about the allocated travel-time and bring us back on the correct route to achieve our destination, especially if we have meandered off our goal-track for a while. This meandering is common, because Life will naturally throw other things our way (**remember the John lennon quote about' life is what happens to you, whilst your busy making other plans').**
These life-issues**, will** now require us to spend our focus, energy, skill and time (FEST) dealing with them. However, because we will have to deal with these other life-issues, then this normally results in our time and energy being distracted for a while, and so we meander off our goal-track.

However, if you have an 'expected time of arrival', and you have placed a 'Finish-time', on each SWEATY goal, then your mind will keep reminding you that the timer is running down, and this helps to re-motivate us forwards again into action, and get back on the correct road towards the desired destination.

Y= Stands for 'YOU'.
Finally, I said to the boys (who I could see where all beginning to get really bored),
the 'Y' in SWEATY stands for 'YOU'.
SWEATY goals have to be about 'YOU'. What YOU want and what YOU are going to do.
Too many people make the mistake of creating GOALS in which other people have to change, in order to make their lives better. If you make your GOALS about what someone else wants or needs to change, then we have little influence over achieving these GOALS because we cannot control what other people do with their energy, skill and time.
But, we can control how we spend or our own time and energy, as well as what attitude, work-rate and ambitions we can focus on.

I finished this session, by telling the young football players, about a male tennis player that I once worked with, whose coach had asked me to help him, as he felt, he wasn't training as hard and didn't appear as focused as he should be, before his big final match. So when I asked him about what his goals for the match final were, he said; well I hope it starts to rain because my opponent doesn't like the wet surface as much, I hope the crowd cheer me the loudest as my opponent doesn't like being the least favourite on court, and I hope he gets a few bad calls from the umpire as he gets annoyed easily and his game slips when he is annoyed. I smiled and said, I asked you about your SWEATY GOALS, not your opponents fears. He quickly realised why he hadn't been as dedicated to training as he could be, because he was spending too much of his minds energy and time focusing on his opponents Game and not enough focus on improving his own GAME.

This always reminded me of the Voltaire quote' *Too many people spend far too much time staring and commenting on other people's gardens and not enough time cultivating their own'.*

Technique 2: create a visual image of each SWEATY Goals and repeating looking once a day.

So, the final part of the session was to teach the boys a technique for creating 1 SWEATY goal that did not link to their football, but that they would like to achieve one day in the future (a future ambition). Then I got them to search the internet and find an image or a video-scene which would link as a visual to seeing their SWEATY goal, basically helping them to create a vision board of their SWEATY Goal. In order to help get them get in a more ambitious mood for the class exercise, of creating an ambition for the future, then I played them the song, called 'Rockstar' by Nickelback.
The music did not seem to be successful at lifting their ambitions.

I then brought out large Jar and I had small and large rocks on the table.
I asked the boys 'which rocks should I place first in the jar', they all answered 'the small ones',
So I did this, and then when I tried to pour all the large rocks in, then they would not fit in the jar.
I then emptied the jar and now placed the large rocks in it first. Then now, when I poured the small rocks in they began to filter down through the spaces between the large rocks and eventually I could close the lid on the Jar. I told the boys that this exercise was like planning their SWEATY Goals, they should start by writing or visualizing their Big SWEATY Goals first and

then work backwards to each of the smaller goals which need to be achieved first, to eventually make the BIG SWEATY GOAL happen.

Then I asked them to put on their mindfulness masks again and close their eyes and I taught them a relaxed breathing technique which was simply entitled, '**smell the relaxing aroma and blow out the birthday candles**'. However, when their breath blew out the birthday candles, then now at the same time they were to imagine getting their SWEATY Goal, just like they were receiving a gift on their birthday.

Then they would simply, look at this visual of their **SWEATY** goal at least once a day.

Usually In bed before they fell asleep and or just after they just woke up in the morning.

This was to help push the images deeper into their mind, causing them to be stored easier and recalled quicker in order to produce more stimulation of these SWEATY goals in their mind. Watching and thinking about their SWEATY goals before going to sleep at night, would help them get absorbed deeper into their mind as they fell asleep from conscious, to sub-conscious and ultimately into unconsciousness. Doing it again in the morning, when they first woke up, would also help it absorb deeper into their mind as they were awakening out of unconsciousness through sub-conscious and finally conscious mode.

Paulo's SWEATY Goal= To stop eating chocolate
Ishmal's SWEATY Goal= to pass all his school exams
Lennons SWEATY Goal= To Stop smoking (yes, he smoked even though he wanted to be a professional football player)
Aldous= To stop watching Porn (I think he thought this would shock me)
Rocky= Go to the gym at least 3 times per week

In summary, I said boy 'SWEATY Goals help to give your player positive future targets to focus on and try and achieve, which makes your player feel more confident and motivated'.

Whereas if your player is not focusing on positive targets ahead, then he will be focusing on his fears, which are the negative targets which he doesn't want and this will cause your player to feel stressed, anxious and scared (which is not a good combination for a winning performance in the game).

The Problem is that although research has shown, that you are 4 times more likely to score a SWEATY goal if you have actually created one in your mind, however most people if you ask them what their future goal is for the focus, energy, skill and time that they are currently spending in the game, then they don't have one-(very strange indeed, I said)?

I then got them to reflect on how frustrated they had been at the coach forcing them to play very unambitious strategies in their game at the weekend, which cost them their victory,

Well, I said to them 'Life will be always be like that for you boys, if you don't start setting some ambitious SWEATY goals for yourself, then I can guarantee you, that life or other people will come along and set them for you, and those GOALS may not be the one's that you were hoping for in your game.

Then they asked me to total up their fantasy scores awarded from today's class and update the class league table which lay next to their football league table, both of which were hung on the wall and sat below their London Underground 'Game-improvement map'.

As they could see their class results did not mirror their football results, but I smiled and said to them ' **don't worry lads, as there is a still plenty of time left for you to play in the game yet, and who says I am talking about football?'**, but they did not appreciate my sentiments.

Finally, as the bell went and they were all scurrying out of the room 'I shouted to them'

Remember boys, I said, 'You never lose in this game, you only win or you learn'.

Week 2 Fantasy football results

Name	Value	Points this week in game	Total points from all games	Current Rating out of the 22 players
Aldous	30 mill	9	19	1st
Paulo	15 mill	8	17	4th
Rocky	10 mill	7	15	5th
Lennon	5 mill	6	13	11th
Ishmal	1 mill	6	12	14th

Week 2 Fantasy class results

Name	Value	Points this week in class	Total points from all classes	Current Rating out of the 5 in class
Rocky	10 mill	9	19	1st
Paulo	15 mill	7	14	2nd
Ishmal	1 mill	6	12	3rd
Lennon	5 mill	4	8	4th
Aldous	30 mill	3	6	5th

Chapter 9: Attitude Amplifier versus ambivalence

PILAR session 3: Attitude Amplifier versus ambivalence

PILARS LAW 3= *'The law of relativity', states that people will judge if they are satisfied with their game success and happiness levels in life, relative to the people around them, who they spend most time with. We become unhappy when we have less of a game, relative to the other people around us.*

'People do not like admitting that they have changed their minds, but they are happy to say that they have made new decisions based on new information'. -Zig Ziglar

I was pleased to have heard in the staffroom that team A had won again and so I assumed the boys would be happy, but When I entered the coaching classroom, they were all there waiting for me and I could hear them bitching about how unjustly they had been treated with regards their fantasy football scores. Apart from Aldous of course, who was sitting as proud as a peacock, confident in the knowledge he had scored another hat-trick, performed best in the game and won man of the match and had lived up to his reputation and price-tag as the player with most potential. At this rate he would equal the all-time greatest score of 120 points in 12 weeks set by the current England captain-Michael Mumford.

I remember thinking that he had a look about him which said 'God, help the coach who hasn't picked me in their team'.

I told them all 'not to worry about their scores as it was still early days in the game', and I jovially said **'there is a still plenty of time left for you to play in the game yet, and who says I am talking about football?'**, but once again they did not appreciate my Monday morning energy.

Moving forward in our life Journey?

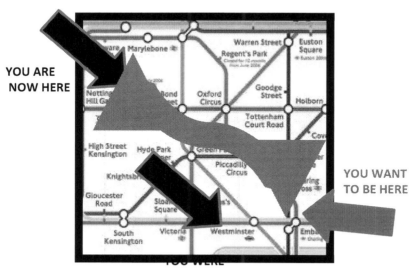

YOU ARE
NOW HERE

YOU WANT
TO BE HERE

YOU WERE
HERE

I then asked the boys if anyone had found the £10,000 treasure box which the head coach Frank had hidden someone in the camp and the clue to its whereabouts was;
'The sooner that you can see the process, then the next part of the journey will unveil itself and the treasure will be found'.

They all groaned "NO".

So, We then proceeded to have our weekly circle meeting, where the boys all had a chance of talking about their highs and lows from last week, before we would start this weeks' session on '**So you think you could be a coach'?**
When I asked about any high points, the boys all started cheering and clapping over at Rocky and chanting his name.
Rocky, was humiliated and went bright red and when I asked him what it was, the other boys just started telling me the story instead. On Saturday their day off, they had all went into town.
When they walked past the local park, they could see a man harassing a woman and her son who had down-syndrome. He was shouting abuse at her and slapping the boy and it was obvious that no-one else who walked past wanted to get involved as it looked like just another domestic situation. However, Rocky had insisted to the others that they go and intervene as it didn't seem right.
After resiliently standing his ground with the man for 5 minutes and arguing with him about his behaviour, Rocky then managed to pull the woman and the boy away and took them to the police station. It later turned out this man was a known paedophile and Rocky had probably saved the young boy from a horrible ordeal in the park. The police had commended Rocky on his community attitude and praised his actions.
I could tell that although the other boys were slagging off Rocky for his actions, underneath they were very proud of having him in their team and they all probably wished that they acted with his tenacity and resilience.

I congratulated Rocky also and said that he showed great attitude to have the strength and resilience to do what he did, and then with a cheeky wink at the boys, I said funnily enough this session is themed around amplifying the 'attitude' of players in your team.

I revisited the alien encounter scenario and asked the boys 'what would you say if the alien came back' and asked you, ' What is it, that makes someone a great player, 'what are the main core ingredients, which determine if someone has the skill to become a top player in your game'.
Aldous, said 'Someone who is focused and can score loads of GOALS', (of course he would say this).
Lennon said, 'Someone who has great speed and Physical fitness levels and can keep giving 100% from the start to the end of the game'.
Paulo said, 'Someone who has great skill, for controlling a ball and changing their direction and pace, to outwit other players'.
Rocky said, 'Someone who understands and reads the game very well, makes great decisions on when to tackle and when to pass to others and can plan ahead for different Strategies, as well as change their tactics against opponents, if things are not going well in the game'.
This was a very good answer I thought, and then I turned and looked at Ishmal as if to say 'your turn', and he just shrugged his shoulders and said 'yeah all of the above'.

I said, 'collectively you have all nailed it', because all the great skillful players that I have worked with, who have been very successful in the game, have all had those 4 main components. They have great **Psychomotor skills** (the ability of your brain to control and program many different accurate and quick muscle responses). They also have good **Physical fitness** (the amount of Physical energy that your body can store and quickly release when required). They have all had knowledge of the best **social tactics and strategies** used in the game. Therefore, they would study their opponents before a game, and plan how best to use their **Psychomotor skill** and their **Physical energy** efficiently in the game. A good plan or set of tactics, should help a team and an individual play efficiently, by maximising their strengths and minimising their weaknesses in the game, (whilst ideally, minimizing their opponent's strengths and maximising the opponents weaknesses).

Finally a great player has a great '**Mindset with Mind-fitness'**, which is the ability to control and focus your mind on the most helpful thoughts, in order to master your 'emotional energy state' during the game. This Mind-fitness, can also help your player to process quickly and accurately what is going on in the external game, so that they can make good internal decisions, about the best way for them to react and spend their Mental, Emotional, Physical and Social (MEPS) energy in the game. This quick processing and good decision making ability associated with Mind-Fitness, also helps a player to perform to their best potential in the game.

But, I said 'which one of these 4 elements (Psychomotor skill, physical fitness, social tactics, or Mindset) do you think is the most important', I asked them?

Paulo said 'are they all equally important professor', good answer Paulo, but not quite right.

Aldous said, 'Skill level', No I said.

Lennon looked at me doubtfully and said 'Physical fitness', I nodded my head from left to right.

Ishmal looked quickly up to the ceiling, as if he thought this would help him disappear from my vision.

Finally, Rocky said, 'I think its Mindset and Mind-Fitness professor, because that is the one that drives improvement in all the others'.

'Absolutely brilliant Rocky', I said, I just knew that this boy would go far in the game.

So, in our first session, we created an **awareness** map and found our current location on the map. In the second session, we then worked out where our **desired destination** was that our **ambition** would like us to be located at instead. Then we worked out, how far away our desired destination is, from our current position.

Therefore, now in order to move forward towards our next desired destination then we need to activate these 4 components of our player.

I got the boys to look up at them =improvement map' on the wall and I said to them;

'Your **Mindset is the equivalent of** how good your **driver** for the journey is, your **Skill-leve**l is how good a **car** you have for the journey, your **Physical fitness** is how much **fuel you have in the tank for the journey**, and your **social tactics** are how good your map or **sat-nav system in the car is,** for helping you to navigate different routes on the map and plan the quickest and easiest path to get you to your desired destinations'.

So, whilst they are all important I said, 'without a good driver then the rest of them can only take you so far on their own'.

But I proclaimed in an upbeat voice, the good news for you 5 players, is that I am here at the summer camp, to try and help you improve your drivers **mind fitness and your game mindset**, and if you play along with me, then this will help you all **travel further in your journey** and become better players in your own game.

They all just looked back at me like zombies in a bad horror film, so I guessed that my wonderful 'journey-car-driver', analogy had completely **travelled** over their heads.

We then started the third session of my certificated course called **'So you think you could be a coach'**, in the same way as we always did, with defining what aspect of Mind-Fitness or Game-mindset that we wanted to help create in our player today.

1= Definition of Attitude

Something has told me that you have all heard the phrase 'That player has a great attitude, whilst others have a bad attitude', but what does it actually mean when your mum or dad, or you teacher or your coach says that 'you have a bad attitude'?

Interestingly enough I told them that the word 'Attitude', comes from aviation terms and means 'the angle of the plane relative to the ground as it Takes off' (as opposed to the 'altitude', which is the height of the plane relative to the ground'). If the plane doesn't have the correct attitude (angle for take-off), then it cannot take off or it will quickly get brought back down to earth again. I could see that my interesting, aviation words of wisdom had yet to take-off in these players minds. I pointed up to their improvement-map on the wall and said in terms of your map, then attitude is the energy that propels you to take-off and move forward from where you currently are, and towards your next desired destination

So how we take-off as players at the start of each game and how high our performance reaches in the game, is very much linked too our attitude.

So, as a mind-fitness coach the definition you will learn in this class is that by, 'a players attitude' and its opposing trait their 'ambivalence', we mean

Attitude= Whether your player currently thinks that the game is important enough and worth it for them, that they are willing to put their skill, energy and time (SET) Into learning and improving it.

Ambivalence= Whether your player currently thinks that the game is not important enough nor worth it, that they are not willing to put their skill, energy and time (SET) Into learning and improving it.

So, you can see boys from this definition, 'that there are many things in life that we can have a good attitude or ambivalence about', depending on how important we think it is and how much of our Skill, Energy and Time (SET), that we are willing to spend on improving our game (our Game-SET)

I am sure that Some of you have a great **'attitude'** when it comes to watching movies or girls, or parties, or the x-box ,or snapchat, but are more **'ambivalent'** towards homework or studying, and so you devote more of your skill, energy and time (SET), to the former (once again my wit was lost on these blasted teenagers).

Anyway, for the purpose of developing your players game today, then as a coach, you need to ask yourself these 2 questions:

1= 'Does your player currently think that becoming a professional footballer is important enough for them to be willing to spend a lot of their skill, energy and time (SET) on developing their game (Game-SET).

2=' 'Does your player think that these 'Mind-fitness coaching' classes could be important enough to help them develop their game, that they feel it would be worth it, to spend a lot of their skill, energy and time (SET) on them, for the rest of summer camp?

I told them to write down their answers to each question, using a score anywhere from -10 to +10

(-10= meant not at all, 0= don't really know either way, (ambivalent) and +10= meant that it was the most important thing in their life at the moment).

This is what they wrote:

	Que 1		Que 2
Paulo;	+10	and	+6
Ishmal;	+10	and	+2
Lennon;	+10	and	+4
Aldous	+10	and	0
Rocky;	+10	and	+10

I thanked the boys for their honest answers and then I told them, 'That it surprised me, that coaches would still ask their players if they were 'motivated to improve their game', because every player that I had ever worked with, had always genuinely answered 'Yes' to that question.

But in reality, this was the wrong question, we should not be asking players 'are you motivated to change'?, but rather the real question to any player should be, 'are you motivated enough, that you are now willing to pay the cost of the journey required, in terms of spending enough of your skill, energy and time, to move you forward to the next desired destination in your game?".

I told the boys that 'If the answer is 'No, then you end up like Lennon and get kicked off the train journey, before reaching where you want to be'. They all turned and laughed at Lennon, as they recalled him trying to dodge the fare on the London train.

With earnest I said, 'In Life, the cost of any journey forward, is measured in how important it is to you and therefore how much of your Skill, Energy and Time that you are willing to spend, to get to the next desired destination of your game.

I then asked them to look up to the improvement map on the classroom wall.

As these 5 young players, looked up at their names on the map on the wall, and saw where they were on the map and read the scores of how far away that they thought this was from where they would like to be instead. Then I wondered, if for the first time in their lives, they had a chance to ask themselves that very important question before you start on any journey forward?

'Is moving towards that next desired destination, important enough to me just now, that I am motivated and willing to pay the cost of the journey, that will help me move forwards towards reaching the next desired destination in my game?".

2=Why is a great 'Attitude', important in helping your players game performance?

So, I asked them all the question, 'Why do think that a great 'Attitude', is important in helping your player put in their best potential performance?

Paulo said= 'So that they turn up for training each week and listen to the coaches tactics'.

Ishmal= 'So that they train as hard as they possibly can'.

Lennon= 'So that they listen to the coaches after the game about their performance and what they could improve upon, for their next game'.

Aldous= 'So that they want to develop even more skill than everyone else'.

Rocky='So that they keep going on the pitch, even when their muscles are tired and in pain and it would be easier for them just to give up and relax, but their attitude keeps them going.

All great answers, I replied.

'Yes, the better the attitude that your player has, will mean that they will devote more skill, energy and time (SET), into the planning and training stages before their game starts (pre-game attitude). Then a player with great attitude, will also believe that it is important enough to win the game, that they will be willing to keep their energy levels going on the pitch, despite their muscles feeling tired and in pain and discomfort. A player with a great attitude, will keep going, as long as there is still time left to run in the game (present game attitude). Finally, a player with fantastic attitude, will still want to find the time and energy to put in a critical reflection of their performance afterwards, as they know, that it is important to keep improving and developing their performance after each game (Post-game attitude).

If your player truly wants to give themselves the best chance to keep winning and developing their game, then they need to see it as having these 3 stages; 'Pre, Present and Post game''.'

Therefore I said to the boys, as a coach 'a player with great attitude is willing to spend their skill, energy, and time in each stage of the game, in order to give themself the best chance of scoring a goal in the game, getting a winning result for their team and to continually develop their game for improvement.

Alternatively, I told them, 'if you as a coach find that your players have ambivalent mindsets, then they will not train as hard, or play right up until the end of the game, or reflect on their performance to improve for the future game'.

'Why'?

because all of these things take up their Skill, energy and time and their lack of game-mindset, will just tell them that it is not worth spending it on.

To prove my point, I told them the story that I had once spoken to the coach of the world's current best player, (they all knew who this was). I had asked him, about the players attitude and had it changed now that he was a superstar.

He replied by telling me, 'that he was always the first player to arrive early in the morning to training, the hardest working competitive player at training, and after training had finished, well he still stayed on longer than anyone else did'. And he still is doing it to this day.

There was no doubt in my mind, that it was this attitude, that had helped make him such a great player and had kept him playing the game to the highest level, even after so many years.

3=Where does your attitude come from, and how do you get it?

So, I asked them this question, 'as a coach, if we know that 'a good attitude', is so important to how well your player can perform in the game, then where do you get your attitude from?

Paulo said= 'You get it from your coach', (he obviously thought, that this was the answer I was hoping to hear).
Ishmal= 'You get your attitude from the media', (he had been reading too many marketing theories).
Lennon= 'You get it from your opinions' (yes Lennon, but where do you get them from?)
Aldous= Grinned and said 'You get your attitude from your parents'.
And I replied 'Aldous, you are more correct than you think and yet most parents with belligerent teenagers would like to believe that you couldn't be more wrong'.
My funny clever quip was once again lost into the ether.
Rocky= 'Professor, you get your attitude from the experiences that you have already had in your life, and how you have processed these and reacted to them', (I was starting to believe that this boy, would become a great therapist, if he didn't make it in football).

Okay I said, 'Your all correct, in that your attitude to anything (how important you think something is), can be gained from many different influences or sources'. Your attitude comes from a cocktail mix of your memories, experiences, your beliefs, your parents, your coaches and teacher's attitude, your focus, your awareness, your energy levels, your confidence, your opinions and the opinions of others who are influential in your life.
The information your mind gathers from all of these influences, gets processed and stored in your brain, and then it decides based on this information, how important something will now

be to you. It is this level of importance which your mind values something at, which ultimately convinces you how much of your Skill, Energy and Time (SET), that it is worth you spending on it, in your game.

The problem I said 'is that, as you continue to move forward in the game, then new external information, experiences and choices are constantly being introduced into your mind also'. This means that your mind will continue to change its attitude about how important certain aspects of your game are, and thus keep trying to change your view on how much of your Skill, Energy and Time (SET) that you should continue to spend on moving forward in that area of your game.

I told them that one of my favourite Zig Ziglar quotes was that 'People do not like admitting that they have changed their minds, but they are happy to say that they have made new decisions based on new information'.

So as a coach, 'the important thing to remember about your players attitude, is that whatever game you are playing in, you need to convince your player that this game is important enough, to make it worth their while, to keep spending all their skill, energy and time on trying to win it.

To prove this point, I got them to name, some of the professional footballer players that they considered to have the worst 'attitudes', (you know who you are).
Were these not the same players, who only ever thought it important to play their best in the big cup games or 'near the end of their contract renewal date', but would be often be missing in action, if the team were playing some low division team in the middle of nowhere, with very few people watching in the pouring rain?
Conversely, we then discussed and named the players they most loved with the best attitude, those football warriors who 'always gave you 100% on the park in every game, no matter what or who the opposition was'.

Lennon laughed and said 'yeah, they would even slide-tackle their granny if it meant winning'.

I finished this section, with a story about a professional footballer I had been working with recently, who had been playing football out in his back garden with his son on his 6th birthday, as he had bought him a new football kit and ball. I said to him, 'surely you let your son win on his 6th birthday', and he joked, 'no way, I couldn't do it, I still had to beat him'.

I smirked and said, 'I guess some great players, just get so good at nurturing an important attitude to every game, that winning becomes such a habit for them, that they find really hard to break'.

4=How do we assess, if our player has the correct level of attitude before each game?

So in the last section, 'We worked out that as a coach, the important thing to remember about your players attitude, is that whatever game you are playing in, you need to convince your player that this game is important enough, to make it worth their while, to keep spending all their skill, energy and time on trying to win it (game-SET).

So, my next question to you all is, '**As coach, how will you assess, if your player has the correct level of attitude before each game?**

Here were there answers:
Paulo said= 'You get it from the effort they have put into training that week', (as usual, he obviously had been talking to coaches).
Ishmal= 'You ask them what they know and think about the opponent's strengths and weaknesses' (He was good at doing his pre-game research).
Lennon= 'You get it from their confidence, energy and enthusiasm in the dressing room', (Yes Lennon, but some people with a good attitude, still like some mental quietness before a game).
Aldous= 'You get it from asking them how good they are going to feel and how much they are going to celebrate, when they beat their opponents', (He was always thinking of the pleasure in the post-game).
Rocky= 'Professor, you ask them about how important it is for them, to play their best and win this game, and if there is anything that they feel, could stop them from being able to put all their skill, energy and time into this game', (This boy was a natural born coach).

Great, I said 'once again collectively, you are all correct in that these are all ways to measure someone's attitude before a game'.

You get it from the physical effort they have put into their training before the game. You get it from the amount of time and thought that they have spent on studying their opponent and planning on the best way to play them. You get it from their confidence, enthusiasm and positivity about being able to play in the game. You get it from knowing that they have visualised all the enjoyment of celebrating the victory afterwards, as this helps them to believe that all the skill, energy and time that they will have to spend in the game, will have been worth it, at the end. Finally, yes you get it from asking and listening to them, about how important they think that spending their skill, energy and time on winning this game is, and if they feel that they currently have enough skill, energy and time to spend on winning this game. You also ask them, if there is anything else currently going on for them, which could stop them from being able to devote all their skill, energy and time into this game.

I finished this section by telling them the story of the Sportswomen who had decided to try and complete a marathon.

She had trained so hard, but the day before the marathon, her daughter took seriously unwell, but she decided to run anyway, as she had been doing really well in her training. However, on mile 23 out of the 26.2 miles, when all her physical energy was gone, and she needed her positive mind-fitness energy to keep her going for that last 3 miles, then she told me, it had all disappeared, because it had been used up that day and the day before, thinking and worrying about her daughter. If only, she had learned the techniques that I will show you today then she could have converted this negative mental energy into positive mind-fitness instead, and she would have been able to complete the final 3 miles of her race successfully.

Moving forward in our life Journey?

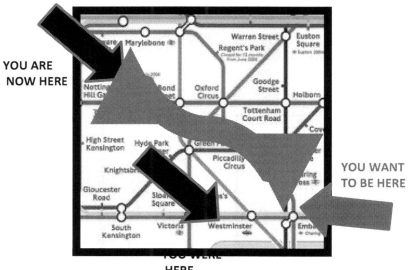

YOU ARE NOW HERE

YOU WANT TO BE HERE

YOU WERE HERE

5= What techniques can we use, to help to change our players level of attitude (increase it or decrease it).

So, in our last section we worked out as a coach,' **how to measure if our player has the correct level of attitude before each game'.**

So ,my next question to all of the boys became, '**As coach, if you have worked out that your player does not have the correct level of attitude you require for the game, then how can you help them improve it, before the game starts?'**

In order to help them do this, I asked them all to close their eyes and focus on trying to recall anything that they had ever thought, or heard, or seen, or physically experienced in the past, before a game began, which then negatively affected their ability to play well in that game and they had their worst game ever..

I then got them, to repeat the same exercise, but to now recall things which they had ever thought, or heard, or seen, or physically experienced in the past, before a game began, which then positively affected their attitude and helped them to play their best game ever.

After the initial chaos of each boy sniggering from self-consciousness, and then each of them opening their eyes, to see if everyone else had their eyes closed (why do young people all do this?), then eventually we got some good responses to the exercise.

I asked them to keep their eyes closed as they recalled the things which had a negative and positive effect on their attitude and performance from any of their previous games.

I always found that people could recall things from their past more vividly and powerfully when their eyes were closed. This was due to the fact that approximately 70% of the information that our conscious mind decides to focus on and process, is linked to what we are externally seeing through our eyes. Therefore, once we close our eyes, then we have 70% more mind power to focus on doing other things with our mind, like accessing more of our feelings and memories, visualising our goals, finding solutions to our problems, or to generate new exciting ideas for using in our future games.

I joked and told the boys, 'that is why all meditation begins with closing your eyes and it is also why, everyone who meditates, looks more happy and intelligent'.

I could see that they were not convinced.

Here were the answers that they spoke out loud whilst their eyes were closed:

Paulo said= 'The Negative effect on me, was the time that I heard the opposition crowd laughing and booing at us when we played in a big cup game, at the same time I had remembered overhearing my dad saying to my uncle in the car before the match, that we would never be able to beat these opponents. I felt let down by his lack of belief. I played very badly in that game and can't even remember touching the ball'.

The Positive effect, 'was the time that I scored and played awesome in training one week, that earned me the 'man of the match' and loads of praise from my coach. I then, went into the Saturday game with great confidence and won 'man of the match' again, which was the first time that I had ever won this in a competitive game'.

Ishmal= 'The Negative effect on me, was the morning when my mum and dad split up, they were always arguing and fighting a lot. But one morning my dad was still drunk and shouting at me for something pointless, when my mum just kicked him out, saying it was the last straw. I blamed myself for causing this to happen between them, and I was not feeling great because I had hurt my knee the day before also. However, when I told my mum about how I was feeling, she shouted at me and then cried, and then told me just to go away and play in the game anyway. I played really badly in that game and gave away the goal that got us put out of the cup'.

Positive effect 'was the time that I was made captain by the coach one week, as our usual captain was ill. I was worried, that the role would be too much for me, but the coach told me that he had total faith in me, to make the rest of the team play well. It was our team's biggest victory of the season that week scoring 12 goals and conceding none'.

Lennon= 'The negative effect was the time that I played really badly in training the day before a cup final. The whole team slagged me off in the changing room afterwards, and I couldn't stop thinking about how embarrassing it was and what if I played like that again in the cup final the next day? By the next morning of the cup-final, my confidence was so low and I then played equally bad in the cup final and we lost'.
Positive effect, 'strangely enough was the week after my grandfather had just passed away, he had attended every one of my games and was my biggest fan. So, after he died, I didn't want to play football for a while. But my mum and dad, told me just to go and play and make the game a tribute to him. Well, I ran about at full speed and full of confidence for the whole of the next game as I felt my grandfather was still there watching me. I scored the winning goal and it was probably the best, that I have ever played in a game'.

Aldous= 'The negative effect was the time that I was not picked by the coach to start an important semi-final game. When I finally got on the pitch, there was only 20 minutes left to play and the game was already lost, so I had little chances to score in that game. I left the team after that game'.
Positive effect 'was getting told that our junior cup final was to be played at old Trafford in front of the England manager. I scored a fantastic overhead goal that won that game, and I got my shirt signed by the England manager'.

Rocky= 'The negative effect was the time that I was playing in this game and the guy I was marking had been throwing insults about all day at me. This was made worse by the fact, that he had been playing brilliant and had been skinning me alive with the ball as well. I couldn't focus on my football because of my frustration, anger and embarrassment, and finally I lost it and lunged at him with a two-footed tackle. I was instantly sent off, and just after that, my team then lost 2 goals and got beaten. I felt guilty and that I was too blame'.

Positive effect 'was getting told by the coach, in my first game as captain, that we needed to beat our next 6 opponents in a row, in order to win the league that year, however the coach felt this was impossible. Well, I decided to try and prove him wrong and for the next 6 games I played out of my skin, winning 6 man of the matches in a row. I also motivated all my team-mates before and during each match with a song, which I had created, which was very vulgar towards our opponents, but very catchy and good fun for us to sing in the changing room before each match. The song, definitely seemed to unite us and helped everyone play better for those last 6 matches. Needless to say, we won the league that year and I won team-player of the year'.

'Fabulous', I exclaimed with far too much energy, and they all quickly opened their eyes from their little journey into football-meditation.

Once again, I said to them, 'just like a bunch of buddhist monks, you have pretty much discovered what things, that our mind can use to either help improve our attitude or ruin it.

I asked them if they had also noticed how different the energy levels within their body had felt as they recalled the 2 different memories (1 negative and 1 positive). Surprisingly enough, all 5 of them quickly nodded and agreed.

Yes, I said' it is amazing how different is the 'energy' that is produced by each of these positive and negative mind-sets. Finally, you have all experienced, how these different emotional energies, then created very different performances from you in the game'.

These situations which our mind focuses on, then dictate our attitude going into the game, and therefore how our performance will take-off at the start of the game and how high or low our performance will reach in the game.

In summary, From this little exercise I said, ' we have learned that the following can make our attitude worse and our performance worse; 'being socially laughed at or booed, people not believing in us or giving us a chance, being physically in pain or emotionally hurt and sad, previous experience of doing badly which lowers our confidence, Being excluded from playing, being made to feel foolish, angry or insulted'.

Whereas, 'the things which helped to improve our attitude were; 'previous experience of doing really well and being awarded or complimented for it, as this increases our confidence and makes us want more. Being given a unique responsibility for motivating or helping others and for someone to have faith in us to do this role well. The chance to perform for a big prize, or in front of an important audience, or to show someone how much you love them, or just for a shot at personal glory. Feeling united with others against an opponent or united in an important cause and finally and strangely enough, for people not to believe in you and so they give you an important incentive and reason for wanting to prove them wrong'.

So, 'I hope that you have learned today boys, that people can always change their attitude, if they are given enough reasons to make a game more important'.

As a coach, then you can always help change your players attitude, if you can give them powerful enough reasons to think that this game is important, and why they will personally gain from playing their best in it. If you can do this, then your players will now be willing to spend more of their skill, energy and time on winning the game for them, and you, and the team.

I pointed back to the map up on the wall with their 5 names on it, and I said that 'Your attitude is what will produce the energy, that will propel you up into the air and help you fly from your current location to your next desired destination'.

Finally, I asked the boys, 'If they had noticed that they had put 'people not believing in them' into both the positive and negative attitude list?
I then posed the question to them, 'Does this mean that things which can improve your attitude, may also have the ability to decrease your attitude?'
I could see that they all looked puzzled, but this was an important aspect of attitude, that I wanted them to understand, as it was linked to a future session that I had planned for them. The lesson was simple; 'Everything can make your attitude better or worse depending on which way you focus and process your view on it'.
I then told them the story about the 2 golfers I had worked with. Before teeing off together in the final round of a Major championship, they both got the news that one of their heroes (a golfing legend), had just passed away.
One of them went on to shoot a great round and won, whilst the other shot one of their worst rounds ever in a major tournament.
When I asked them both, what they had been thinking about and focusing on the whole way round the course, one replied 'how sad it would be that I would never see my golfing buddy ever again; and the winner told me ' how happy I was that I got to spend time playing in a beautiful game with him and I imagined he was still with me at every hole, smiling and telling me how well I was doing in the game'.

Next, I told the boys that 'I was now going to teach them a technique, that I had originally created for helping people beat addictions'.
I told them that this was a quick, simple and easy technique but if repeated, was a wonderfully powerful way of making something like a SWEATY goal, become more important to your mind. Once it is made more important, then this will convince

your mind, to devote more of your skill, energy and time into getting it, or will help you to be able to endure more sacrifice and discomfort for longer, in order to help you achieve the goal.

The technique I showed them was simple'. They would all lie down in the 'Plank position'. This is because we need to train ourselves, to find better ways of improving our attitude, therefore making something, even as simple as 'the Plank exercise', to become more important to our mind, so that it would help us, to keep going for longer, through the pain and discomfort of the exercise.

Technique 3: The Plank with Focus on important thoughts
So, in the plank position and initially with their eyes open, then I got them to keep going until they got to the 'failure' point (when they could no longer hold the plank position). I recorded each of their timings before they gave up the exercise, and Aldous did the best with a time of 1 minute 55 seconds.

I then played them the song " you can't always get what you want' by the Rolling stones and got them to repeat the exercise another 5 times, but each time they would now focus their mind on thinking of their SWEATY Goal from the last session, and then I wanted them to link their SWEATY goal to one of the 5 powerful and hard-hitting suggestions from the list, that I had made below. Once again, I timed each of their 5 efforts, in order to work out, which type of motivational suggestion, would make their plank seem more important to them, and therefore, help them to work hardest at this exercise and spend more of their skill and energy and time on it.

The 5 motivating ideas that I wanted them to focus on and link to their SWEATY GOAL, whilst doing the plank exercise were,
1= If you kept going, then it would help you win 1 million pounds

2= If you kept going, then It would make someone of your choosing fall in love with you or allow you to spend more time with a loved one who is no longer here.

3= If you were now doing it in front of a large crowd of people chanting your name, and you would become world champion if you manage your best time.

4= If Your worst enemy was laughing at you and saying that you couldn't keep it going.

5= If your life (or someone else you love) life depended on it.

The boys were all energized after their 5 attempts, and the exercise seemed to have gone well, as they all saw improvements in the length of time that they were now capable of being able to do the plank exercise. They all done very well and each of them improved their results with each new focus. It was the first time since I had met them, that I had the feeling, the boys were beginning to appreciate and understand the powerful role that their mind could play in improving their game performance.

I finished this class, by telling them of my work with 'a certain professional boxer, whom I had trained to program his attitude, by always using this technique, as soon as he heard the bell at the start of each new round'. After I taught him to do this, he became well known for coming out at the start of each round like a caged tiger.

Their homework for this week, was to repeat this quick and easy 'Plank' exercise, every night and each morning, at the same time when they were also visualizing and focusing on their SWEATY goal.

However, now they were to focus their mind whilst doing the Plank, on coming up with new motivating reasons (no matter how ridiculous), for making this Sunday's game really important for them to perform well in. They would say and repeat each suggestion out loud and record their time doing the plank. This I told them, 'will ensure that before the big match on Sunday, you will have worked out, what idea is best for coaching your own inner-player into having the most important attitude possible for the game'.

I told them that each journey forwards, requires you to focus and spend your skill, energy and

time up-front, before you take-off and reach your next desired destination.

I gave them this parting shot, 'Always remember boys, that as a coach, then you can always help change your players attitude, if you can give them powerful reasons to think the game is important enough, to make it worth their while, spending all their skill, energy and time on trying to win it (game-SET). If you cannot do this then it will fuel their ambivalence levels for not really caring about performing to their best for themselves, you or the team.

I then turned to Rocky with pride and said, 'unlike the ambivalent others in the park, because of your great attitude on Saturday Rocky, when you decided it was important enough to put your skill, energy and time into intervening. Then you managed to stop a young boy from being seriously harmed'.

'Well done Rocky' we shouted and we all clapped to him in unison, (but of course being a teenage boy, this was to his complete horror and dismay).

I then awarded them their fantasy class results from week 3 and wrote these on the league table on the wall. As they could see their class results did not mirror their football results, but I grinned and said to them ' **don't worry lads, as there is a still plenty of time left for you to play in the game yet, and who says I am talking about football?'**.

Then as the bell went and they were all flying out of the room 'I shouted back at them'

Remember boys, I said, 'You never lose in this game, you only win or you learn'.

Week 3 Fantasy football results

Name	Value	Points this week in game	Total points from all games	Current Rating out of the 22 players
Aldous	30 mill	9	28	1st
Paulo	15 mill	8	25	4th
Rocky	10 mill	7	22	5th
Lennon	5 mill	6	19	11th
Ishmal	1 mill	6	18	14th

Week 3 Fantasy class results

Name	Value	Points this week in class	Total points from all classes	Current Rating out of the 5 in class
Rocky	10 mill	9	28	1st
Paulo	15 mill	7	21	2nd
Ishmal	1 mill	6	18	3rd
Lennon	5 mill	4	12	4th
Aldous	30 mill	3	9	5th

Chapter 10= Finding Focus versus destroying distraction

PILAR Session 4: Finding Focus versus destroying distraction

PILARS LAW 4= *There are 6 main groups of thoughts which we can focus on, which have the power to change our emotions or physiology. These 6 groups lead to 6 groups of emotions which lead to 6 groups of behaviours which lead to 6 groups of social interactions.*
So be careful about which group you are focussing your minds time and energy on.

Change your focus, and you will change your feelings and this will change your future
Alan Curley.

So, it was Monday morning class again and I had already had a sneak preview in the coaches staffroom of their fantasy football scores from Sundays fourth competitive match.
The boy's team had lost on Sunday so I expected them to be in a low mood this Monday morning. However, to my disappointment, I had also heard that there had been a lot a drama that weekend. As always, I had left campus at the weekend to go visiting old friends from my study days in Oxford, so I never got to see the boys over the weekend or watch them play in their Sunday football game. The boys were allowed off campus every Saturday as they were given a day-off from training and this was meant to be a treat for them to get away from their dormitories and see some new surroundings. However, a coach had told me that some of the boys from Team-A had went into town on Saturday and returned back to campus extremely drunk that night. To my dismay, 4 of these

boys were in my class (only Paulo had stayed away from going on this booze-cruise). The coaches had already had a 'dig' at me this morning in the staffroom, asking if I was teaching these boys 'drinking games' in class, instead of teaching them 'mind-games'. Even though it was annoying to hear them laugh about the Sports mind fitness and game mindset work I was doing, I did take comfort from the fact that I hadn't taught the boys their class on 'staying Focused' yet, but coincidentally that would be their treat for today.

Once again myself and the 5 boys sat in our 'truth circle', and I asked them to tell me about the drinking incident and how it had affected them, in terms of the high and the low points of their week. Not surprisingly, the low point was that they had lost their game on Sunday. I wanted them to take responsibility for their role in the loss, so I asked them the question, 'Did they think that their loss on Sunday was linked to the majority of their team being hungover', or did they think that losing the game, was merely an unrelated universal coincidence!!!

I should have known better, but stupidly enough, they all thought that it was just a coincidence, as they felt they had played just as good as they did in the first 3 games (yeah right).

The story they told me was that 'on Saturday by some strange turn of fate, they had ended up in a local pub (in fairness, some of these 16 year old boys did have beards and were built like 40 year old men). When they were in the pub, then a group of local lads, had challenged them to a 'shots' competition, and by 'shots' they didn't mean kicking a ball (yeah I got that lads). Needless to say Aldous was at the centre of it and whilst most of the boys were willing to refuse and ready just to go home, Aldous worked his manipulative magic using a combination of peer-pressure and knowing that most of them had a competitive streak in

them, and convinced them all to take on the local lads in a drinking game. However, despite being 16 year old sporting heavyweights, they were still 'alcoholic lightweights' and 2 hours later they had lost the game. By the time that they had arrived back at camp, they were absolutely hammered and most of them spent the night 'puking' their own body weight in tequila, zambooka and jaeger-bombs.

I asked them 'whether during their practicing of the technique that I had taught them in a previous class of visualising the one SWEATY goal that they wanted to see happening at their big final match day here in camp'. 'Did any of them visualizing getting drunk before the game as a helpful aid to them achieving their SWEATY goal at their final match'?

Furthermore, I asked them 'what was more important to them (ATTITUDE), to get drunk last Saturday or to achieve their SWEATY goal at the final big match here at camp (AMBITION). I told them that , 'just like most bad TV gameshows, you can't walk away with both prizes in this game'. You have to choose which prize is most important to you (ambition and attitude) and then focus on achieving the SWEATY GOALs which will take you to this next desired destination of your journey.

Well I said, 'this brings me nicely along to the fact, that we are starting session 4, today of your certificated course',

'So you think you could be a coach?".

This course will take you further into becoming your very own great personal coach and to develop your best player possible.

This week, luckily enough we will be learning how to increase your players focus and concentration on their goals.

After Saturday's shenanigans, then this is obviously something which most of your players have lacked up until now (I nodded over to Paulo, in recognition of the discipline which he had shown this weekend in this department). At the same time, Aldous uncomfortably looked away, Ishmal went a red-colour that I have never seen anyone go before, Lennon timidly laughed and Rocky looked like he was going to start crying and beg for forgiveness.

Anyway, it's over now I said, and like most games, we pick up ourselves and learn from it, so that we play better next time.

Remember boys, I said, 'You never lose in this game, you only win or you learn'.

They really hated this condescending, upbeat mantra of mine.

1= Definition of Focus

So, I said to them all 'Something tells me, that you have all heard the phrase 'You need to focus more on your game' but what does 'Focus' actually mean?

So, as a mind fitness coach the definition you will learn in this class is that when we talk about your players 'focus' and its opposing trait 'distraction' we mean

Focus= The ability to keep your minds energy concentrated for a prolonged period of time, on one specific thought or task that you have deliberately chosen.

Distraction= The ability to let your minds energy drift and wander away for a prolonged period of time, to numerous thoughts that it chooses for you.

So you can see boys that so far in our course **"so you think you could be a coach"** we have covered;

-**Attitude** was making something more important in the present, that you think it is now worth spending your skill, energy and time on getting better at it.
-**Ambition** is wanting to and move forward and achieve more in your future
-**Goals** are those specific things in the future, which you need to have scored or gained from the skill, energy and time that you will have spent in the game, in order to reach your ambition.
-**Focus** is being able to keep your current mental energy concentrated on one specific thought or one task for a period of time.

I asked them what they would think if I told them that I knew a blind-striker who plays in a disability league and is top scorer. They all proclaimed 'surely, his Inability to see ahead and therefore to keep focused on the ball and on the target, would make it difficult for him to score goals'.

'Yes, your right' I said, 'you would think that the inability to be able to see where you are, or to be able to keep looking ahead and stay focused on your target, would make it harder for anyone to score their goals.'

However, I said, 'he manages to overcome this disadvantage, by tuning into his other senses in the game, and increasing his awareness of vocal cues from his team-mates'. He also has to keep reminding himself every minute to re-orientate himself back to facing the goal-net, so that if an opportunity does arise to score, then he knows that he is facing in the right direction, to hit the target. This means, that he has to have total concentration during the game, in order to keep bringing his focus back to doing this every minute. If not, then he will lose sense of which direction he is heading in, and when he does get the ball, he will not know which way to strike it, thus losing out on the opportunity to score the goal.

I told them that this blind-striker often jokes that, 'he is the proof, that it's easier for a focused blind man with a target in front of him to score a goal, than it is for a fully-sighted man to score, who doesn't have a target to aim for, or know which direction he wants to be heading in.

2=Why is 'Focus', important in helping your player perform better in the game?

So, In our inner circle of wisdom, I asked them all the question, Why do you think as a coach, that helping your player to have better focus, will help them play better?

Paulo said= So that they want to keep learning and getting better at the game (this was his answer to everything).

Ishmal= So that they can follow the game and their opponent better

Lennon= So that they can keep their eye on the ball at all times.

Aldous, = So that they know what the score is and if they need to up their game.

Rocky= 'Professor, is it so that they always keep reminding themself of the coaches tactics for the game and their own personal SWEATY goal and why it is important to keep trying their best until the end of the game (this boy had definitely been listening in class).

All of you are correct, I replied.

Yes, 'the more we develop our ability to stay focused, then the more mental and physical skill, energy and time that we can devote to any task for longer. Which usually means that we do it better and a lot more successfully.

When our mind does wander (which it inevitably does), then improved focus helps us to become more aware of our wandering, and this helps us to bring our focus back quicker, more frequently, and for longer periods (recall the blind striker having to re-focus himself and re-orientate himself every minute of the match). Keeping focused in the game, will keep us running for longer, we can follow the team tactics for longer, we can concentrate and stay aware of what Is happening in the game for longer. Focus helps us to keep a watchful eye on our opponents for longer and watch the ball for longer. Focus helps to keep reminding you of what your Team goal and your own personal SWEATY goal is, and why it is important to keep going and keep performing to the end of the game, even when your monkey-mind is trying to tell you that you are tired and your muscles are in pain. On the other hand, distraction helps your mind wander away quicker from the conscious world and therefore wander away from your conscious tasks of keeping up with your opponent and the ball and on keeping to the teams tactics and strategies. Therefore, distracted players spend more time out of the game than focused players. That is why they are less successful in the game.

I then told them about the darts player that I had worked with, who would often start his matches very well, but his form would dip in the second half of his game. I had carried

out some focus tests with him and it was obvious that his problem was all down to the fact he couldn't focus as long on his game-plan and staying calm, as most of other players could. I showed him the technique that I am about to show you today and within weeks his focus and concentration during his performances had improved significantly and so had his world rankings In the game.

I then pointed back up to the map on the wall and said that 'focus was the ability for each of your drivers to stay driving on the road, but to also keep their eyes on the sat-nav system in the car and understand how to read it, therefore they have the ability to keep driving ahead and stay on the easiest quickest direct route towards your desired destination. Whilst distraction, was the ability of your driver to not fully understand how the sat-nav system works and be frequently forgetting to look at it, therefore constantly going off on detours and wring roads and away from the desired destination. This ultimately means that it takes a lot longer and is a lot more expensive for a distracted driver to reach where they want to be and hinders their chance of ever getting there in time.

Furthermore, there are 2 types of focus, just like seeing in darkness versus seeing in light. Your mind can focus its time and energy on powerful negative adjectives (Fears or problem-focus)' or powerful positive adjectives (goals or solution focus).

I told the young players that it is important to remember that 'the mind will devote its time and energy to finding the answers to the questions and thoughts that you either allow it to wander into or that you specifically give it to focus on'.

'Therefore be careful, because you will experience more of the feelings related to what you allow your mind to keep focused on'.

That is why saying 'why am I stressed' is not helpful, because your mind doesn't process the word don't, but rather focuses itself on the powerful word 'stressed'', and so it will now spend more of its time and energy answering your question by making you think about all the things which make you stressed'.

Whereby, if you had said to your mind, 'I wonder what could help me relax and enjoy this situation more', then your mind will be more focused on this helpful question and thus spend its time and energy on finding you solutions ' to what things make you relaxed and enjoy things more'.

Or if someone says to themself 'why am I fat, and why can't I stop eating CAKE'. Then they have focused their mind on the words fat and cake, and their mind is now spending its time and energy answering their question 'why am I fat' and why can't I stop eating cake', both which keep it focused on creating lists of depressing reasons of why you are fat and love cake. Whereas, saying ' how can I get thinner or what foods will help me lose weight', would have triggered their mind to focus it's time and energy on a more helpful question, which would create in them helpful strategies to help them get thinner and think of better foods that they could eat' in order to aid them losing weight.

I asked the boys if that made sense, and then all nodded their heads in bored agreement, I could see that after all this talk of food, that they were now itching for a dinner-break.

3=Where does your Focus come from, or how do we get it?

So, where do you get your focus from, I asked the boys

Paulo said= You get it from your coach (once again he obviously thought, that this was the answer I was hoping to hear)

Ishmal= You get it from studying the game .

Lennon= You get it from meditating (a budding buddhist monk)

Aldous= once again proclaimed 'You get you it from your parents, as they are always nagging you to focus more at school'.

And as usual I replied 'Aldous once again you are correct, focus just like many skills can be trained into you by your parents. Parents and coaches, who have a lack of focus, normally pass this gift onto their children also.

Rocky= 'Professor, you can get it from brain training exercises which you can use to get your mind to stay focused on items for longer (that sounded like a popular TV gameshow).

Well done, I said once again all your answers fit nicely to the question.

The Monkey-mind and the Master mind

'Focus, just like awareness and ambition are what they call master-mind traits', I told the boys.

Whereas fear and distraction are considered monkey-mind traits. Master-mind traits are your modern evolved higher conscious mind abilities and like most mind-sets these skills can be trained and improved over time, just like all your conscious Physical football skills have been trained and improved since you were young.

Whereas monkey-mind traits are the more ancient unevolved subconscious mind abilities which link directly to our internal physiological systems. These are also very useful but need to be controlled by the master-mind for optimal performance. For instance, you would not have the horse controlling where the carriage goes or you may never get there.

As a coach, you can help your player to focus longer on tactics, through teaching discipline and making tactics more interesting. You can then develop your own focus through repeated studying of these tactics and repeating saying them back again to yourself. Yes Lennon, using mindfulness and visualizing techniques for taking information deeper into your mind will definitely help improve your focus also. Our parents ability from an early age to teach us through rewards and punishments to improve our concentration on things like counting, memorising animal names and noises in a farm, singing songs, learning nursery rhymes, reading stories to us and sitting doing our homework with us, have all contributed to the level of focus you have today, 'or not Aldous,' I said as I caught him daydreaming out of the window.

Finally, 'there are many master-mind- training focus games out there to help you improve your concentration skill, and I will show you one of these later. In fact, some psychologists say that you should give a name to your monkey-mind and your master-mind so as to personalise them more to you and so that you can recognize them better and talk to them sometimes (they all scorned at this idea). So I asked them one by one around the circle to make up names for their monkey-minds and master-minds, respectively.

Paulo said his were 'Juan' and 'Jesus',

Ishmal said his were 'Navran' and 'Gurang',

Lennons was 'Bob' and 'Gertrude' (they all laughed),

Aldous was 'jack and victor'

and finally Rocky's was 'Jimmy and Mary' (after his grandparents).

I got the sense that the boys had not taken this exercise too seriously. But I thought maybe one day in the future they might understand its importance and revisit it with more of a sense of purpose and who knows it may be of use to them.

Moving forward in our life Journey?

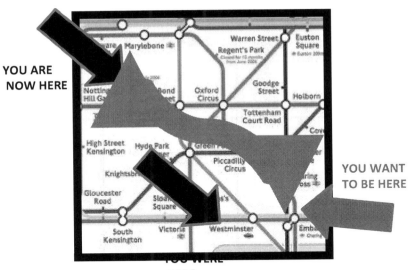

**YOU ARE
NOW HERE**

**YOU WANT
TO BE HERE**

**YOU WERE
HERE**

4=How do we measure if our player has the correct level of Focus before each game?

So as a coach, the important thing to remember is that your players ability to focus, will mean they can concentrate for longer on Your tactics, their own personal SWEATY goal that they wish to achieve in the game, their awareness of what is happening in the game and to keep reminding themselves, why its important to keep trying to win (attitude) and to keep spending their time and energy staying committed until the end of the game (ambition).

So my next question to all of them became '**As a coach, How do would you measure if your player has the correct level of Focus before each game?**

Here were there answers:

Paulo said= You get it from the effort they have put into training that week (that's all he ever says, obviously his coaches have done a great job on him)

Ishmal= You ask them who they are marking and how they will best do it?

Lennon= You get it from asking them what they know about their opponents.

Aldous (without any effort or focus said)= 'You get it from asking them how many goals they think they are going to score this week?'.

Rocky= 'Professor, you ask them to repeat the team tactics back to you again and what their specific role is in these tactics. And you ask them what their personal SWEATY goal is for the match (another excellent answer from the prodigal son)

Well done, I said 'these are all ways to measure your players focus before a game'.

You get it from the physical effort they have focused into their training before the game. You get it from the amount of thought they have spent on analysing their opponents strengths and weaknesses and how well they hope to perform.

You get it from the specific level of detail that they can repeat back to you about the team tactics and their specific role in those tactics and you get it from how specific and detailed they can describe their personal SWEATY goal, so that we know they will stay focused to keep playing in the game right up until the final whistle blows.

I told them about a golfer I knew, who always was more relaxed and shot better in the first 9 holes, but because of this, then he always put pressure on himself to do as well in the back 9 holes. This added pressure in the back 9 holes, and often made him play a lot worse.
This is a common problem in Sport, where the inability to deal with increased stress or pressure causes a decrease In focus. Anyway, we worked on an alarm-sensor technique (which I will show you next), where his focus on the back 9 holes was brought back to the level it was in the first 9 holes, (by getting him to pinch his ear whilst repeating the 9 times table before each tee-off in the back 9 holes). It seemed to work a treat and he won his first major competition that year.

I then asked the special 5, 'if we want to keep our focus during a game, then what are the groups of thoughts that we want to keep our minds focused on during a performance".
Paulo said= You focus on what the coach told you to do before the game (his 'coach' answer to everything)
Ishmal= You focus on what your doing well in the game
Lennon= You focus on what your not doing well in the game, and improve it
Aldous= 'You focus on the great celebration that your going to have after scoring the winning goal in the game.

Rocky=You focus on the personal goal and the team goal which you had before the game.
Well done, I said once again all your answers fit nicely to the question.

The SUPER-6 sets of thoughts

Next, I told the boys that there are 6 very important groups of thoughts which your mind can focus on. These are super-sets of thoughts because they can all generate a change in your emotional and Physical energy in either a positive or a negative way. To change how we feel, then we can either focus our mind on negative and Positive memories from our past (failures or glories), or we can focus our mind on what negative or positive issues we are experiencing at present (problems or pleasures).Finally, we can focus our mind on what negative or positive things could possibly happen to us In the future (worries or wishes). The problem is that if we allow our monkey-minds to decide for us which of these groups it will focus our mental energy and time thinking about, then it may choose the wrong groups, or it will constantly get distracted from one group to another, which in turn, can cause a rollercoaster-ride effect on our mental and emotional energy. Therefore, we need to learn to train our master-minds, so that we get to choose more of the time, which group of thoughts that are best for us to focus our mind on in any given situation. We can also train our master-minds to become aware and quickly return to the more helpful groups of thoughts, when our monkey-mind has made us wander off to other unhelpful groups.

The 6 groups are:

Past-Negative
Past=Positive
Present-Negative
Present-Positive
Future-Negative
Future=Positive

I tried to summarise by saying 'each of these suoer-6 sets of thoughts are probably just like people you all know' (I could see them sit up in anticipation of something more exciting coming next). To clarify I this, I said 'we all know someone who always keeps talking about bad things which happened to them in the past they all nodded and shouted **'Davie',** (who apparently was another footballer in their team).

In addition, 'We all know someone else, who always keeps talking about all their past glories', the boys all turned, smiled and looked at **Aldous,** he was not happy and told them to 'shut up'.

Furthermore, 'We all know someone who is currently moaning about the present situation', they all in unison said **'our parents'** and laughed. 'We all know someone who is always really talking positive about the present', they all laughed and pointed at me and said you **Professor,** (they found it strange that I took this as a compliment). I then said 'and we all know someone who is always worried and fearful about the future', they all chuckled and pointed at **Ishmal,** (and he was aware enough to nod and smile back in agreement).

Finally, we all 'know someone who is always talking about their dreams and hopes and goals for the future', they all shouted the name '**Rocky'** (and embarrassingly rocky agreed).

So now we have 6 classroom names for our super-6 set of thoughts and I mapped these up on the wall. If I hear any of you speaking in certain positive or negative ways from now on, then I will know you are either in:

Past-Negative is Davie-mode,
Past=Positive is Aldous-mode,
Present-Negative is Parents-mode,
Present-Positive is Professor-mode,
Future-Negative is Ishmal-mode
Future=Positive is Rocky-mode.

I started laughing as I looked up at this mind-map on the wall, that we had created with the different super-6 names. However as I looked around the classroom, Aldous was still sneering with contempt at it.

Moving forward in our life Journey?

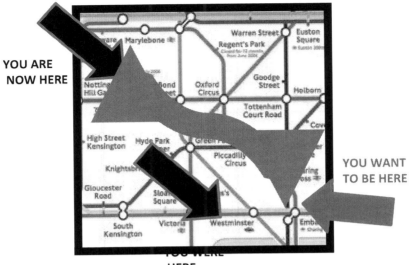

YOU ARE
NOW HERE

YOU WANT
TO BE HERE

YOU WERE
HERE

5= What techniques can we use, to help to improve our players level of Focus.

So now I will show you all a coaching technique for being able to Focus better and activate your Master-Mind and control your Monkey-Mind

This technique also helps you to train your focus levels, as it gives you a Physical tool for choosing when to alter your thoughts, which will help to alter your feelings, which more importantly, will help you to change your performance behaviours and the results you can get In the game.

Technique 4: Activating Alarm sensors

The technique is called 'alarm-sensors'. It is similar to Pavlov's dogs stimulus-response method.

This technique allows us to use our 5 senses as an alarm system, to activate our focus back to a specific helpful thought, which we already know, creates a specific energy change within us (happy, motivated, confident). I reminded them of the exercise that we previously did when they were recalling situations, which had made them play their best or worst games in the past.

Furthermore, this tool helps us to activate the alarm for wakening up our master-minds, which is useful for when our monkey-minds have caused our focus to dose-off sleeping in the game.

I asked them, if they had ever noticed, 'a footballer running on to the pitch before a game starts, and you see them Tapping their watch, or had they ever noticed that certain football players if they are not playing well, stop and pull both their socks up (this is called a metaphorical alarm-sensor). Or had they noticed that before a performance certain athletes will taste a particular chewing gum, or smell their glove, or listen to a song, or look up to the heavens or look at a photograph, or touch their wedding ring Or twist around their necklace or kiss their jewellery, (Aldous laughed and shouted 'kiss their ring, sir''?).

Well, you can probably bet that it has been me, who has taught them to do this 'alarm-sensor' technique, in order to focus their master-minds back onto a specific thought using their different senses.

And now I am going to teach it to you.

An 'alarm-sensor' is a tool for creating or recalling a single thought in your mind, which you wish to keep your mind focused on, as it will be helpful to you in a specific situation and will act as an alarm for awakening your focus and energy levels. The thought can be from any one of the previous **super-6** sets of energy changing thoughts; negative and Positive memories from our past (failures or glories), or negative or positive thoughts about what we are experiencing at present (problems or pleasures), or negative or positive thoughts about our future (worries or wishes). You then choose one thought from each of the **super 6** sets and link it to one of your senses. For example you link smelling a Particular perfume to focusing your mind on a future SWEATY goal, or you link hearing the song 'eye of the tiger from the film rocky' to a present pleasure' In your game or you link saying a certain phrase to the memory of a past glory, or if you see the colour red ,then it will remind you of a future worry which motivates you to try and avoid.

The focus back onto these specific helpful thoughts during the game, will be triggered like an alarm system by your corresponding sensory processes, whenever they see or hear or smell or touch something which you have programmed them to remind you to focus on. So, there is often no need to have to consciously remember to do them.

'Why is this so important', I asked the boys, 'Well it is because our monkey-mind gets easily distracted and forgets important thoughts like our tactics and strategies, when we are in the heat and battle of the game. Our monkey-mind also becomes distracted by the fact we are feeling physically tired or our muscles are in pain, or that we are in emotional stress and it will begin to focus all your attention on these unhelpful things. Once this happens, our monkey-minds internal priority of what to spend its mental energy and time focusing on changes and so we forget the important tactics and SWEATY goals that we had trained pre-game and focus more now, on how tired our muscles are feeling or the pain we are in, and so our monkey mind decides to give up.

However, the alarm-sensory technique gives us an alarm clock for wakening your master-mind back up to focusing on the strategies and SWEATY goals which you and the coach had installed during the training sessions. I asked them to remember the story of the blind striker repeating this every minute, so as to remember to re-orientate himself back to facing towards the goal.

I have taught many coaches to set up an alarm-sensor with their players, which involves tapping their watch in the last 10minutes of the game and when they see the coach doing this, then the players are reminded to re-focus themselves and keep going, because they still have time left to win or lose the game.

The simple beauty of this technique I said boys,' is that if you pick powerful, yet subtle enough sensory alarms, then you can repeat this technique anywhere or anytime. By activating each sensory alarm, then you will get your master-mind to focus your mind back to a specific idea during the game, that you had already pre-programmed to be important and helpful to you before the game. This technique acts like an alarm system for programming your future mind to be able to get re-focused back to an important thought that you had set up in the past.

I joked and told them they could now be just like Dr. Who, and be capable of taking their minds on time-travel because thoughts from their past self can now talk to thoughts from their future selves (once again this clever analogy was not understood and they all stared blankly and pathetically back at me).

I then got them all to set their own alarm-sensors for refocusing their master-mind up to the one personal SWEATY goal which they each hoped to achieved by the end of their time at the 12 week summer camp. To aid this sensory processing within their minds, then I played the song by john Denver called' Annie's song'. I hoped it would help them.

I then placed a heart monitor and blood pressure monitor on to each boy and I asked them to close their eyes and begin to think of one thought at a time from each of the super-6 sets of thoughts.

After each thought, then I got them to open their eyes and see the difference in their Blood pressure and heart rate levels, depending on whether they were thinking of a negative thought versus a positive thought. Then I used an ultrasound device to get them to listen to their blood flow supply in their arm. When I asked them to tense the muscle in their arm versus relax the muscles, then they all heard the changing ultrasound noise linked to their blood flow. Depending on whether their muscles were stressed and tense versus the more calming flowing sound when their muscles were relaxed. I told the boys 'that these exercises were to prove to them, that we all perform better in the game when we are in a relaxed positive confident state and we perform worse when we are tense and negative and stressed.

Stress can be okay for a short while, but if you begin to be chronically stressed then it really affects your performance in the game. I told them of the current research that has been done in adverse childhood experiences (ACE's), that children being brought up in environments of toxic stress and often chronic stress, have now being show to have many more physical and mental health problems in the future, because of this chronic toxic stress. But many people are putting themselves in these chronic and toxic stress states also, because they are spending too much time focusing their mind on the 3 negative groups from the super-6 and these 3 groups (Past-Negative, Present-negative and future negative), all trigger the stress response within us. Spending the wrong amount of time in each of these 3 super-set groups is the leading cause of why people are in therapy nowadays.

To prove this, then I had got some small arm weights from the gym and I asked the boys to each lift a set of them and hold them straight out,' Are they heavy' I asked, they all laughed and said 'these are girls weight sir,' but I said I want you now to keep holding them up and outwards and let's see if they start to get heavier over time. Their smiling faces dropped, and within 4 minutes, the last of them had lowered their arms in agony. You see boys, it is often not the weight or level of the stress which is overwhelming or hard to burden, it is the amount of time that you have been carrying it which eventually takes its toll on you in the game.

It is also the same for these ACE's children who are constantly living in these environments with adverse experiences and therefore experiencing continued chronic toxic stress.

I then gave them homework which was to keep activating their alarms every 5 minutes in the game this week, so as to bring their focus back from their monkey-minds and into their master-minds.

Paulo used the sensory smell of mint chewing gum (he always chewed when playing football),

Ishmal used the sensory tapping of his watch,

Lennon used seeing the colour red (he was a manchester united fan)

Aldous used 'kissing his biceps'

And finally Rocky used hearing the song 'always look on the bright side of life' from the monty python film 'the life of brian'

As I was writing their fantasy class scores up on the wall next to their fantasy football scores then I asked the boys if anyone had found the £10,000 treasure box which the head coach Frank had hidden someone in the camp and The clue to its whereabouts was;

'The sooner that you can see the process, then the next part of the journey will unveil itself and the treasure will be found'.

They all groaned "NO".

The boys also moaned about their class scores and pointed out that their class results, did not mirror their football results, but as I always said to them

'Guys, there is a still a lot of time left for you to play in the game and who says that I am talking about football!.
-This hilarious statement always drew me gormless looks back!!!!

I wished them good luck for this match Sunday and then said the famous phrase
Remember boys, 'You never lose in this game, you only win or you learn'.

Moving forward in our life Journey?

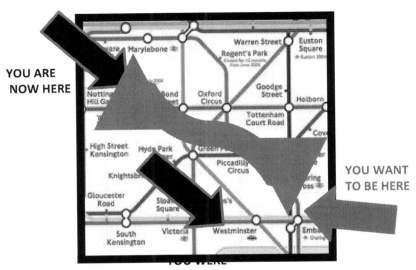

YOU ARE
NOW HERE

YOU WANT
TO BE HERE

YOU WERE
HERE

Week 4 Fantasy football results

Name	Value	Points this week in game	Total points from all games	Current Rating out of the 22 players
Aldous	30 mill	9	37	1st
Paulo	15 mill	8	33	4th
Rocky	10 mill	8	30	5th
Lennon	5 mill	6	25	11th
Ishmal	1 mill	6	24	14th

Week 4 Fantasy class results

Name	Value	Points this week in class	Total points from all classes	Current Rating out of the 5 in class
Rocky	10 mill	9	37	1st
Paulo	15 mill	7	28	2nd
Ishmal	1 mill	6	24	3rd
Lennon	5 mill	4	16	4th
Aldous	30 mill	3	12	5th

Chapter 11= Manufacturing Mind motivation versus expelling excuses

PILARS LAW 5= *Every chemical change requires a catalyst (Awareness change) and a spark of energy (motivation) and time for the reaction to proceed. Every change will produce a waste product which is given off during the reaction. However, most reactions are reversible if you do not keep applying the right amount of energy for the right amount of time or if you take the catalyst away.*

'Of course motivation is not permanent. But then, neither is bathing; but it is still something you should do on a regular basis."
Zig Ziglar

Monday morning class was here again, and it felt that every week went quicker. I remember when I was younger, an uncle of mine, telling me that every 10 years of your life goes quicker than the last 10 years. I never thought much of his statement at the time, but I now see that his prediction has very much came true in my life.

As per usual, I had already checked out their fantasy football scores from Sunday's week 5 game. I had also updated their scores on my fantasy mind-performance table, based on their engagement in the class and with the quality of their alarm-sensors which they had performed in the last session.

They were always quick to point out that their class performance results, did not mirror their football results, but as I always said to them

'Lads, you still have plenty of time still to play in the game and who says that I am talking about football!.

This statement was always met with a huge groan

This week when I entered class, they were all whispering and giggling like schoolgirls. This meant that there must have been some gossip from their Saturday shenanigans. Like most good therapists, then it wasn't too hard or too long before I had managed to get them to tell me everything, once we had sat down in our usual circle at the beginning of class. Apparently, they had been in the town on Saturday and had came across a group of girls form a local residential private school. They had charmed these young woman and had eventually got to kissing them and getting 'dates' with them next Saturday. I was almost amazed at how confident and energetic some of these young men where, until it came to talking to the fairer sex and then they became bubbling, babbling, lethargic self-conscious idiots.

They had also Won their football match, which showed that the arrows of love had not affected their football skills (yet!).

They must have all been 'love-struck' this week because they all told me that there had been no low points to their week (I seriously doubted that, but then love is blind).

For the first time in 5 weeks, they actually commented on how useful using one of the techniques that I had showed them had worked. I was very much happy to hear that they were now beginning to use and find my techniques helpful, although unfortunately, they had not used the technique on the football field. They joked about how their 'pulling' of the fairer sex, had all been down to 'my alarm sensory technique', which I had showed them in the previous class'. When I asked why ?, Aldous replied' because Paulo and Ishmal weren't

Week 5 Fantasy football results

Name	Value	Points this week in game	Total points from all games	Current Rating out of the 22 players
Aldous	30 mill	10	47	1st
Paulo	15 mill	8	41	4th
Rocky	10 mill	8	38	5th
Lennon	5 mill	6	31	11th
Ishmal	1 mill	6	30	14th

Week 5 Fantasy class results

Name	Value	Points this week in class	Total points from all classes	Current Rating out of the 5 in class
Rocky	10 mill	10	47	1st
Paulo	15 mill	8	36	2nd
Ishmal	1 mill	7	31	3rd
Lennon	5 mill	4	20	4th
Aldous	30 mill	3	15	5th

going to go and talk to the young ladies, but then aldous had convinced them to set up an alarm-sensor with the SWEATY goal that they would end up getting 'Sweaty', with these girls.

Although their intentions were extremely questionable, at least I was comforted with the fact that they had remembered to practice their homework technique. Strangely enough, they had unintentionally used it in a relevant situation to help them alter their emotional energy and confidence state for an improved performance. I proceeded to tell them that their love-heroics was very topical to this week's session Because today in session 5 of your certificated course, **'So you think you could be a coach?".**

We want to follow on from the last session by asking the question 'How do you get yourself motivated enough to turn your thoughts into action'. So, this week, luckily enough we will be learning how to increase your players motivation and to help them to spot excuses which are stopping them from achieving their SWEATY goals.

I could see the boys were all riveted to hear about this theme.

I asked them to recall for me the definitions which we had used from last week of focus (master-mind) and distraction (monkey-mind). Rocky, piped up with definitions that were almost perfect. He proudly said 'Focus and distraction, in this class are defined as:

Focus= The ability to keep your minds energy concentrated for a prolonged period of time, on one specific thought or task that you have deliberately chosen.

Distraction= The ability to let your mind drift and wander away for a prolonged period of time, to numerous thoughts that it chooses for you.

Excellent I said, Rocky you have a great awareness, attitude, ambition and focus which means you will reach your goals in life.

All the other buys laughed and Rocky went bright red.

'Did you see what I did there', I said to them but they all looked back at me with that dull teenage blankness.

I proudly exclaimed that I had summarised all our sessions to date, in a compliment to Rocky (and now they looked back at me, with a sense of pity).

In your certificated course 'so you think you could be a coach'. We have covered:

-Ambition= wanting to become better and add more to your future

-Attitude=making something more important in the present, that you think it is now worth spending your skill, energy and time on improving it.

-Goals= those specific things in the future which you want to have scored or gained from the skill, energy and time that you will spend In the game.

-Focus= being able to keep your current mental energy concentrated on one specific thought or one task for a period of time.

1= Definition of Motivators, maintainers and reversors.

I said to the boys 'Something tells me, that you have all heard the phrase 'Stop giving me excuses and just get motivated to get it done'.

But what do the words 'motivators' and its opposing skill 'maintainers' actually mean?

So, as a mind fitness coach there are 3 definitions you will learn in this class related to the effect that thoughts can have on our journey of change (and I pointed up to the map on the wall). Thoughts can act like motivators (and move you forward), or maintainers (keep you where you are), or as reversors (move you backwards to where you have been before).

Motivators= The ability to focus your mind on thoughts that increase the emotional energy within you and trigger a forward change.

Maintainers= The ability to focus your mind on thoughts, which convince you not to spend your skill, energy or time into making a change and therefore help you to stay where you are.

Reversors= The ability to focus your mind on thoughts, that can alter the emotional energy within you, but which trigger a reversal backwards to past behaviours.

I kept pointing to the map on the wall and said basically, 'motivators give you the energy to move away from where you currently are and move forward to a future desired destination. Whereas maintainers convince you to stay at your current location, and reversors convince you to leave where you currently are and go backwards to a previous location on your map.

So you can see boys in terms of your map up on the wall, then so far we have covered;
-**Awareness** is knowing where you currently are on the map and how far away that is from where you would like to be.
-**Ambition** is wanting to move forward in the future, to another desired destination.
-**Goals** are the travel route-plan of those specific places that you need to reach first, which lie between where you are and where your desired destination is.
-**Attitude** is thinking it is important enough now, to leave your current location and commit spending your focus, energy, skill and time moving on to reach your next desired destination.

-Focus is being able to keep your mind concentrated on staying on the correct route to your next goal.

-Motivators are the fuel which keeps you moving forward on your route to the next desired destination.

I told them that 'motivators, maintainers and reversors, are all opposite ends of the same spectrum. They can alter your willingness to spend your skill, energy and time in the game. One makes you want to spend them moving forward (motivators), the other wants to spend them where you currently are (maintainers), and the final one wants to spend them going back to a previous location (reversors).

I then finished by telling them about the 2 college basketball players that I had worked with, both of them were angry young men had been suspended for 6 games for fighting on the court. One of them used the 6 weeks to party as he couldn't play anyway and the other used the 6 weeks to motivate himself to learn to control his anger. One of them got offered a professional contract the next year and the other didn't.

2=Why is 'Motivation' important in helping your player perform better in the game?

So, In our inner circle of wisdom, I asked them all the question, 'Why do you think as a coach, that it is important for you to help your player to become more motivated when playing the game?".

Paulo said= So that they listen more to their coaches (no surprises with this answer).

Ishmal= So that they enjoy being a player in the game.

Lennon= So that they turn up with a positive attitude for the training sessions before the game

Aldous, = So that they look forward to the victory of winning the game

Rocky=So that they can keep themselves focused on what is important in the game and keep replenishing their energy for playing in the game, this will help them to keep learning and getting better at playing the game (I remember thinking that I could easily adopt this intelligent young man).

Well done, I said once again all your answers fit nicely to the question.

Motivation helps us to want to learn more about the game from our coaches, as well as keeps us enjoying the fact that we are a player in the game. It also helps us to think positively about the hard work and training that we need to put into developing our game. Motivators also keep us reminded of the pleasure of the future spoils when we get a victory in the game. Finally, motivators keep us focused on the helpful groups of thoughts which can increase and regenerate an energy within us, which we can then invest back into developing our game, and keep playing the game for longer. If we do not have motivation then will begin to see training and developing our game as a chore, and then we will keep losing our energy in the game and before we know it, we will get tired of playing the game and no longer want to be on the field.

3=Where does your Motivation come from, or how do we get it?

So, I asked each of the boys, 'where do you get your motivation from'?

Paulo said= I get motivation from my coach and watching other professional players on the TV.

Ishmal= I get it from reminding myself of how it felt when I didn't play well in the past, or how I will feel if I don't play well in the current game and then telling myself that your future career will not be great if I don't keep playing well and getting better at the game (he obviously learned these words and thoughts from his father).

Lennon= Nervously laughed and said 'I get it from my parents 'nagging' me all the time to do better'.

Aldous= Proudly stated 'I get it from wanting to be the best and most successful player in the game, and thinking about the loads of money I will be earning, the fancy sports cars that I will be driving and the big house with beautiful girlfriends that I will have.'

'Excellent answer Aldous', I said to his dismay.

Rocky= I get it from thinking about what positive things I have done in the past, what I am currently grateful for and what future goals I want to achieve.

Brilliant, I said, you are all beginning to turn into great young coaches.

Yes, 'motivation comes from coaches and role-models who you aspire to be like, it comes from your parents who believe that you can achieve more than you currently are. Aldous is correct also, because you get motivation from imagining all the great advantages that success in your game would bring if you work hard for it.'

Finally, 'both Ishmal and Rocky are correct, that you can get negative motivation from being fearful of the things that have not went well, are not going well and may go badly if you do not keep focused and keep putting your skill, energy, time and effort into your game. Or you can get positive motivation from focusing your mind on the past successes that you have achieved in the game, what you are currently grateful for in the game and what future goals that you hope to score in the game.

4=How do we measure if our player has the correct level of Motivation before each game?

So as a coach, the important thing to remember is that your players ability to become and stay motivated, will mean that they will enjoy playing the game more, which means that they will have more Energy to use in the game, which in turn, will help them to keep their mind focused for longer on the important tactics and strategies for winning the game.

So it is important for players In the game to be able to stay **focused** on the coaches team tactics **(using alarm sensors),** as well being routinely reminded of their own personal SWEATY goal that they wish to achieve in the game. They also need to keep their **awareness** of what is happening in the game and to keep reminding themself why it is important to keep staying committed to trying to win **(attitude)** and to keep spending their time and energy until the end of the game **(ambition).**

So my next question to all of them became '**As a coach, How do we measure if our player has the correct level of motivation before each game?**

Here were there answers:

Paulo said= 'You get it from the effort they have put into training that week' (that's all he has ever said, obviously his coaches have done a great job on him).

Ishmal= 'You get it from how happy they look before the game'.

Lennon= 'You get it from asking them how important it is for them and their team, to win this game'.

Aldous, without any hesitation said= 'You get it from asking them how many goals that they think they are going to score this week?'.

Rocky= Professor, 'you ask them to repeat the team tactics back to you again and what their specific role is in these tactics. And you ask them what their own personal SWEATY goal is for the match. Then you ask them to show you an alarm-sensors that they have programmed for keeping their focus on motivating thoughts during the game.

(I couldn't have put it better myself, I thought)

Brilliant , I said 'these are all ways to measure your players motivation before a game'.

The effort they have put into their pre-game, how happy they feel about playing in the current game, how important it is to them that they and their team play their best in this game. You get it from asking how well they think that they will perform in the game, and you get

It from asking them to focus on what is important about their personal and team role in the game. Finally, you ask them what alarm-sensors they have set up to keep bringing their focus and energy back to all these motivating ideas, whilst playing in the game.

5= What techniques can we use, to help to improve our players level of Motivation.

Technique 5: Motivational Pinch Points

So, our coaching technique for improving motivation is a technique called 'Motivational Pinch points'. The boys looked at me like I was crazy, but I continued, 'In this technique we use repeated Physical pinching to link to one specific motivating thought or memory that we have. We then repeat pinching that area of our body whilst only focusing on our one motivating thought. After rounds of repetition of this pinching, then your mind will now be programmed to instantly think of your motivating thought as soon as you repeat the 'pinch' on yourself. Therefore during your game, when you repeat the physical 'Pinch', then your mind will recall to you the thought which motivates you most to keep going.

Common areas for the pinching to take place are your ear, wrist, thumb or thumbnail, nose-ridge, chin, or knee.

This technique also helps to improve focus as it gives you another Physical tool for choosing when to alter your thoughts to more motivating ones, therefore helping to alter your feelings, which more importantly, helps you to change your performance behaviours and the results you can get. To prove this, I got the boys to all put on a set of drunk glasses (the lenses where designed to make your vision blurred and focusing a lot harder). Then I got them to drive a remote-control car around a few obstacles in the room, as well as carry out other easy tasks of lifting and moving things and taking them around the room.

After the hysterics had finally ceased, I said to them' this exercise was just to show you that when your focus isn't right, then you will not perform anywhere near to the level that you can in the game.

I then got them all to set their own 'Motivational Pinch points' and to link them to one motivating thought that if they focused on, would help give them more motivation in any game situation that they might find themselves in. That way if they were stuck in the middle of a game and having maintainer thoughts or reversor thoughts, then they now had a technique for re-focusing their mind to motivating thoughts which would push them forward again. To help them with this exercise I played them the song 'I've got the power', by Snap. They were not impressed with my music choices.

Paulo pinched his ear and focused on his motivating thought.
Ishmal pinched his wrist and focused on his motivating thought.
Lennon pinched his nose-ridge and focused on his motivating thought.
Aldous half-heartedly pinched his chin and focused on his motivating thought.
And finally Rocky 'Pinched his knee' and focused on his motivating thought (later on in his career, this would become his signature move in a game when he wasn't playing as well as he could)
I told them their homework as usual was to keep repeating practicing the technique before the game on Sunday and wished them good luck for this match.

I asked the boys to look up at their map again and I said 'These motivating thoughts were the equivalent of stopping at a petrol station on the journey and refueling the energy of your car, so that you can now move forward again to the next desired destination.

I asked the boys if 'anyone had found the £10,000 treasure box', which the head coach Frank had hidden someone in the camp and The clue to its whereabouts was;
'The sooner that you can see the process, then the next part of the journey will unveil itself and the treasure will be found'.

They all groaned "NO".

Then I proceeded to award them their fantasy class scores for this session and I wrote these up on the wall next to their fantasy football scores then

The boys also moaned about their class scores and pointed out that their class results, did not mirror their football results, but as I always said to them

'Guys, there is a still a lot of time left for you to play in the game and who says that I am talking about football!.

-This hilarious statement always drew me gormless looks back!!!!

And as they all went scurrying out of the classroom I shouted back to them **'Remember boys, 'You never lose in this game, you only win or you learn'.** They loved to hate me saying this.

Moving forward in our life Journey?

YOU ARE
NOW HERE

YOU WANT
TO BE HERE

YOU WERE
HERE

Week 5 Fantasy football results

Name	Value	Points this week in game	Total points from all games	Current Rating out of the 22 players
Aldous	30 mill	10	47	1st
Paulo	15 mill	8	41	4th
Rocky	10 mill	8	38	5th
Lennon	5 mill	6	31	11th
Ishmal	1 mill	6	30	14th

Week 5 Fantasy class results

Name	Value	Points this week in class	Total points from all classes	Current Rating out of the 5 in class
Rocky	10 mill	10	47	1st
Paulo	15 mill	8	36	2nd
Ishmal	1 mill	7	31	3rd
Lennon	5 mill	4	20	4th
Aldous	30 mill	3	15	5th

Chapter 12= Helpful BELIEFS versus unhelpful BARRIERS

PILARS LAW 6= *Your thoughts are not facts they are just your beliefs or opinions based on the information you have been given and how you processed it, to create your map of the world. However, we can constantly make new decisions based on the new information we receive. Information is processed by the 4 F"s; we can either forget it, file it, forever remember it or forgive it.*
Ultimately, there are only 2 types of belief; those that are helpful to you in moving forward in your game and those that are unhelpful and hinder your game.

'If you make your mind believe it, then you can achieve it'
Alan Curley

When I entered the classroom, the boys were all standing around looking upset and when I prompted them to tell me what was wrong, then they proceeded to tell me that Aldous's gran had passed away during the previous night after a battle with cancer. I looked down at Aldous and for the first time ever, I saw a sincere expression of genuine emotion on his face. My heart went out to the young man, as I knew from conversations with him, that she was one of the few people whom he truly cared for and that had loved him unconditionally in his life.
I could see he from his eyes that he had been crying, but was doing his best to hide it, in front of the others. I then asked him if he wanted just to miss class today and spend time on his own, but in fairness he said in a muffled voice 'No I am alright to keep going'.

I remember always thinking in that moment, that if only I had met Aldous as a child and been given the chance to help him work on his mind-set before his parents ruined it, then he could have been such a truly exceptional human being. He was by far the most naturally gifted young person that I had ever met.

I decided not labor too much on the fantasy football/class league table this week (although Aldous was still ahead of everyone else in the football arena, and Rocky was ahead in the classroom version)

We then proceeded to have our weekly circle meeting, where the boys all had a chance of chipping in about their highs and lows from last week, before we would start this session on **'So you think you could be a coach'?**

This week I decided to ask them if anyone else had experienced someone they love passing away. Only Rocky had experience of death and he helpfully pitched in with a story about his favourite pet dog who had passed away last year at the age of 15 years (much to the laughter of the others, apart from Rocky and Aldous). It was in this moment that I realized again how young these boys actually were. Although they looked physically older and their cockiness made them think they knew everything about the world and how it works, and their futures looked potentially very bright, the reality was that they were still only 16 years old and had not truly experienced the real highs and lows which life inevitably throws at all of us.

I then told them today that we would discuss the helpful beliefs and unhelpful barriers which we can encounter along our journey in the game, and which can hinder our path and send us down the wrong routes, which then require us to find a new route forward.

Because today in session 6 of your certificated course, **'So you think you could be a coach?"**.

We will be discussing helpful beliefs versus unhelpful barriers.

Week 6 Fantasy football results

Name	Value	Points this week in game	Total points from all games	Current Rating out of the 22 players
Aldous	30 mill	10	57	1st
Paulo	15 mill	7	48	4th
Rocky	10 mill	9	47	5th
Lennon	5 mill	6	37	11th
Ishmal	1 mill	6	36	14th

Week 6 Fantasy class results

Name	Value	Points this week in class	Total points from all classes	Current Rating out of the 5 in class
Rocky	10 mill	10	57	1st
Paulo	15 mill	8	44	2nd
Ishmal	1 mill	7	38	3rd
Lennon	5 mill	4	24	4th
Aldous	30 mill	3	18	5th

1= Definition of Beliefs and Barriers

Something tells me, that you have all heard the phrase 'You need to believe in yourself more'.

Aldous looked up, sniggered and said 'no sir,' the others all laughed at his humour especially under his current circumstances.

I smiled also in appreciation, for his willingness to be still involved in class.

but I said 'what do 'beliefs' and its opposing skill 'barriers' actually mean?

as a mind fitness coach then these are the definitions you will learn in this class

Helpful Beliefs= Personal opinions that we have about ourself and others, usually based on past experiences or stories that have been told to us. Helpful beliefs make us feel more confident and that we can move forward towards our goals, by making us believe that we can achieve them.

UnHelpful Barriers= Personal opinions that we have about ourself and others, usually based on past experiences or stories that have been told to us. Unhelpful barriers make us feel more anxious and stop us moving forward towards our goals, by making us believe that we will not achieve them.

I pointed up to the map in the class and said

So in summary boys, so far we have covered:

-Awareness is knowing where you currently are on the map and how far away that is from where you would like to be.

-Ambition is wanting to move forward in the future, to another desired destination.

-Goals are the travel route-plan of those specific places that you need to reach first, which lie between where you are and where your desired destination is.

-**Attitude** is thinking it is important enough now, to leave your current location and commit spending your focus, energy, skill and time moving on to reach your next goal .

-**Focus** is being able to keep your mind concentrated on staying on the correct route to your next goal.

-**Motivators** are the fuel which keeps you moving forward on your route to the next goal.

-**Helpful Beliefs** give you the confidence that your journey will reach the desired destination.

I told them that in my opinion, 'the majority of promising young amateur athletes never make it to the professional ranks, because their unhelpful beliefs make them feel so unconfident, that eventually they convince themselves that they will not be good enough to perform at a high level and that they should lower their ambitions'. This is why so many of them, then turn to junior coaching, at far too young an age, when they could have still been playing and improving their own game.

2=Why are your players beliefs', so important in helping them perform better (or worse) in the game?

So, In our inner circle of wisdom, I asked them all the question, 'Why do you think as a coach, that helping your player to have more helpful beliefs in themself, will make them play better'?

Paulo said= So that they want to keep believing that they can win at the game

Ishmal= So that they will keep committing their energy and focus until the end of the game

Lennon= So that they can stay positive even if things are not going their way in the game

Aldous = So that they can make themselves feel more confident about scoring goals even when they are running out of time in the game

Rocky= So that they always keep positive about playing In the game and can keep picking themselves back up after each defeat or bad performance, as this will nurture their resilience to keep learning and eventually be victorious in the game (this boy was getting better and better).

I congratulated them all on their great answers and I summarized by saying
Yes, 'the more we develop our ability to stay focused on helpful beliefs, then the more feelings of confidence we generate within us. This confident energy then helps us to keep enjoying playing the game and believing that we can do well in it. This belief, then allows us to commit more of our emotional energy and mental focus into the game. Finally, they help us to stay positive and confident to keep picking ourselves back up, even if things are not going our way and we feel that we are running out of time in the game.

I then went on to say that unhelpful beliefs about the past, present or future, trigger feelings of Stress or anxiety or depression. Whereas helpful beliefs trigger feelings of confidence and calmness within us. It is often seen nowadays that many people's games are being affected by stress, anxiety or depression.
Therefore, we need to be able to become aware when we are focused on unhelpful beliefs because there is a certain window of time that we have, before the thoughts will have created their mirror-feelings. The feelings will then be harder to reverse than the thought would have been. We need to break free from the thoughts before they will have triggered the change in feelings. We can do this by re-focusing our minds onto more helpful beliefs about our past, present or future.

I then told them about the football manager whom I had worked with. I helped him create such a powerful belief that him and his team were unbeatable. After a while , other teams and other managers began to think that he had magical abilities to create more time at the end of matches, because

of his teams phenomenal track record of playing with all their confidence and energy right until the end of each game, that they produced many victories from the jaws of defeat usually within extra time.

I told them that I would now teach them these phenomenal 'helpful belief' techniques to pass onto their players.

3=Where do our beliefs come from, or how do we get them?

So, 'where do you get your beliefs about your game from', I asked the boys

Paulo said= You get them from what your coach has told you about the game

Ishmal= You get them from studying your football heroes and knowing what worked well for them in the game.

Lennon= You get them from listening to your friends who play the game with you

Aldous= as usual proclaimed 'You get them from your parents, as they are always trying to get you to believe that what they say and tell you that they are correct. And I replied 'Aldous once again you are correct, beliefs just like behaviours are normally gifts that parents

try to pass onto their children, even if they are unhelpful gifts.

Rocky= Professor, you can get them from your experiences of playing in the game and how your mindset has processed these experiences.

Well done, I said once again all your answers fit nicely to the question. Helpful beliefs and unhelpful barriers can come from your coaches, stories from past players of the game, your role-models, your friends, your parents and from your own mind and your own experiences of how the game has treated you.

I told the boys the story, that when I used to deliver training for staff who worked in addictions units, then I would always start the day with this question to them 'how motivating do you think you are with your clients?'. Most of them would answer that they thought they were very motivating when it came to working with their clients.

I would then ask them the next question?

"what do your clients with addiction feel when they stop their addiction, for example 'what do your clients feel when they stop smoking, drinking gambling or taking drugs?

I was always amazed when they answered ' anxious, stressed, depressed, irritable, bored, fearful and grieving.

And always my reply back to them was; 'No, your clients feel **'bloody brilliant'** when they stop their addiction.

Now, I could always see their surprised looks when I said this, because they suddenly realized that even although they all thought they were very motivating with their clients, their answers were all extremely negative and de-motivating to any potential client wishing to go on a journey of change with them. It was even more surprising because I knew in reality, that they had helped hundreds of people quit addictions and had actually witnessed the great positive change in all of these peoples lives. Yet, this exercise always highlighted, that when I asked them about how people feel when they stop an addiction, their clinical training had taken their minds instantly to negative images and beliefs of the contraindications, symptoms and side-effects of the initial couple of weeks of the journey, and not to the positive images and beliefs of the rewards that you get for the next 40 years.

I then played a game with the boys, that I had devised called 'Bullshit beliefs Bingo'. This is where we all went round the circle and admitted certain beliefs that we have told ourself in the past that were not true and we knew it, but we said them anyway to ourselves, in order to justify our behaviours. I then showed them a video of a whale hologram, which highlighted that our brains react to what we imagine in our minds, rather than to facts or what is actually going on in reality. Finally, I asked them to think about what emotions would be triggered within them, if they spent too much time focusing on unhelpful beliefs from their past, present or future.

I finished by saying to the 5 of them 'it just shows, that many of us focus our beliefs on the wrong part of the journey and this change in beliefs can then change our levels of confidence and motivation for moving on ahead to the next desired destination'.

.

Moving forward in our life Journey?

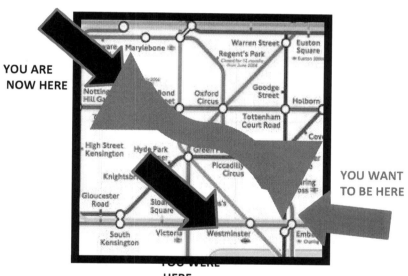

YOU ARE NOW HERE

YOU WANT TO BE HERE

YOU WERE HERE

4=**How do we measure if our player has the correct level of helpful beliefs before each game**

So as a coach, the important thing to remember is that your players ability to **focus,** will mean that they concentrate for longer on Your tactics, their own personal **SWEATY goal** that they wish to achieve in the game, their awareness of what is happening in the game and to keep reminding themself of why it is important to keep trying to win **(attitude)** and to keep spending their time and energy staying committed until the end of the game **(ambition).**

So my next question to all of them became '**As a coach, How do we measure if our player is focused on helpful beliefs or unhelpful barriers before each game?**

Here were there answers:

Paulo said= 'You get it from the effort they have put into training that week' (yeah, yeah, yeah)

Ishmal= 'You ask them if they are worried about anything'?

Lennon= 'You get it from how confident they look in the dressing room before the game'.

Aldous (without hesitation) = 'You get it from asking them if they think their team will win the game'.

Rocky= Professor, you ask them if there is anything that could currently stop them playing to their best potential in this game.

Well done, I said 'these are all ways to measure your players level of focus on helpful beliefs before a game'.

You get it from the physical effort they have focused into their training before the game. You can get it from asking them about their worries or by seeing their confidence levels before a game. You get it from asking them, if they think their team will win the game and you can get it from asking them is there anything that could stop them confidently playing in the game right up until the final whistle blows.

I then told them about a female high-jump athlete whom I worked with, that had received a back injury after an awkward and rare fall onto the bar. The injury had healed, but her belief that the bar would fall on her again, meant that she now froze every time she ran up to the bar before making her leap. Her injury had healed but her belief had meant that her confidence had not healed.
We worked on her unhelpful barriers and installed more helpful beliefs and soon enough she was flying confidently high over the bar again.

5= What techniques can we use, to help to improve our players Focus on helpful beliefs and to break down unhelpful barriers to their performance in the game.

I then asked the special 5, 'if we want to keep our confidence energy levels high during a game, then what are the groups of helpful-belief thoughts that we want to keep our minds focused on during a performance".

Paulo said= 'You focus on what the coach told you to do before the game', (his 'coach' answer to everything).
Ishmal= 'You focus on what your doing well in the game'
Lennon= 'You focus on what you have done well in previous games'
Aldous= 'You focus on seeing yourself victorious and celebrating the win in the game'.
Rocky= 'You set an alarm-sensor to help you keep focused on the personal goal and the team goal which you had before the game and keep repeating to yourself that it will happen.

Technique 6: Eye Movement Desensitisation Reprocessing (EMDR)

Okay I said, 'let's do it then', and I taught them the eye movement desensitisation reprocessing technique (EMDR) that was created by Francine Shapiro.

I told the boys that this technique had been extensively used with war veterans who were still experience post-traumatic stress disorder (recalling unhelpful beliefs and images). Stress and anxiety are caused by unhelpful beliefs whereas confidence is created by helpful beliefs.

The technique is a very effective way of getting your mind to stop focusing on unhelpful beliefs which are causing you stress, trauma, anxiety or depression.

It does this by getting you to close your eyes and think of the stressful thought and how it makes you feel (and score how bad it feels from 1-10)

Then you are asked to open your eyes and keep thinking about the thought but this time you will now create eye-movements back and forth, left to right, which stimulate the left side of your brain and then quickly the right side of the brain. Each time you repeat this and close your eyes then the original stressful image seems to get less clear and less powerful and the score decreases of how bad it now feels.

Finally, you repeat the process but this time you link a really helpful confident thought to the original stressful thought, whenever you close your eyes.

The overall result, is that now whenever your mind tries to make you think of the stressful thought, then you will instantly jump to the helpful confident thought instead.

To help them practice this I played the song 'Don't stop believing' by Journey, and they all practiced this together and were surprisingly very good at trying to dispel their bullshit or unhelpful beliefs from their minds.

I had asked Aldous to think about his grandmother when he practiced this, to see if he could shift his memories of her from emotional sadness to memories and feelings of happiness instead, when he focused on the time they had spent together. He acknowledged to me with a subtle nod, that it had helped, and I was more proud of him in this moment, than at any other time.

I Finished this session by turning to Aldous and saying you know Aldous different cultures have different beliefs about death,
Some celebrate it as the end of a painful chapter and start of a wonderful journey.
Some spiritualist religions believe that you never die, but that your energy is just converted from a physical form into another. Finally, some people believe that you are never dead and you are always alive as long as someone on this earth is still thinking and talking about you. I hope you can focus on whatever beliefs help you Aldous, so that you can focus on the celebrated times that you have had with your gran and not focus on what you will not get anymore. Aldous looked at me with a lost expression, and I remember truly hoping that he could train himself to do this, or else it would become a real problem for his future progress in the game.

I asked the boys to look up at their map again and I said 'These unhelpful beliefs are like bad road signs which send you the wrong way and you get more stressed and more frustrated with your journey going wrong. You will notice helpful beliefs as these are like the signposts which always keep you moving forward happily and steadily to your next desired destination.

I asked the boys this week if 'anyone had found the £10,000 treasure box', which the head coach Frank had hidden someone in the camp and The clue to its whereabouts was;
'The sooner that you can see the process, then the next part of the journey will unveil itself and the treasure will be found'.

They all groaned "NO".

Then I proceeded to award them their fantasy class scores for this session and I wrote these up on the wall next to their fantasy football scores then

The boys as per usual moaned about their class scores and pointed out that their class results, did not mirror their football results, but as I always said to them

'Guys, there is a still a lot of time left for you to play in the game and who says that I am talking about football!.

-I think they were getting tired of this statement.

And as they all went flying out of the classroom I shouted back to them **'Remember boys, 'You never lose in this game, you only win or you learn'.** They never heard it.

Moving forward in our life Journey?

YOU ARE
NOW HERE

YOU WANT
TO BE HERE

YOU WERE
HERE

Week 6 Fantasy football results

Name	Value	Points this week in game	Total points from all games	Current Rating out of the 22 players
Aldous	30 mill	10	57	1st
Paulo	15 mill	7	48	4th
Rocky	10 mill	9	47	5th
Lennon	5 mill	6	37	11th
Ishmal	1 mill	6	36	14th

Week 6 Fantasy class results

Name	Value	Points this week in class	Total points from all classes	Current Rating out of the 5 in class
Rocky	10 mill	10	57	1st
Paulo	15 mill	8	44	2nd
Ishmal	1 mill	7	38	3rd
Lennon	5 mill	4	24	4th
Aldous	30 mill	3	18	5th

Chapter 13= change commitment versus change killers decision-making

Physical PILARS LAW 7= *Life is just made up of a series of choice moments on how you can spend your Focus, energy, Skill and Time in the game. When you commit to changing your game, then You will follow the 4 D's; Do it, Delete doing it, Delegate it to someone else, or Delay it.*

'Every journey starts with a change to your current choices, and the life of your future self will not have improved, if your present self doesn't choose to change.
Alan Curley

When I entered the Coaches staffroom before class, then I could see Frank looking rather worried but the other coaches looking very smug. I instantly knew that my 'special 5', had been involved in something wrong at the weekend.

Frank, looking very sullen and disappointed, told all the coaches that he had found some of the boys smoking 'weed' at the weekend and that they had been keeping it in their lockers.

There was my 5 boys and 3 others from their football team. The other coaches were loving it and making comments like 'Maybe I had given it to them as part of their homework, in order to help them access higher states of their subconscious mind'.

I jokingly said 'of course, that is rubbish, as I would have told them to use LSD instead, Just like Timothy Leary'. However, Frank did not find any of this amusing and became more enraged reminding us all about the prestige and credibility of the summer camp and that the media would have field-day if they found out, and it could jeapordise all the young players future in the game, as well as stop any teams sending their young players here next year. We all apologized, and I said I would have a word with the boys. Frank said that their parents would be informed at the end of camp but agreed that it was best not to inform any of their football teams at the moment as it was an important time in their career.

Before I left the coaches staffroom, I quickly glanced at the wall and noticed that frank was currently sitting top of the coach's fantasy football league. Whereas I, on the other hand was sitting bottom. Aldous was still top of the football league but Rocky and Paulo were moving upwards also. In terms of the class fantasy league then Rocky was still sitting head and shoulders above the rest.

When I entered the classroom, I tried to make my facial features look fumingly angry with a major hint of utter disappointment at the same time. They were all sitting with their faces downwards expecting the worst. I asked them to go around one by one and tell me what made them decide to do such a stupid thing at camp (surely any intelligent teenager would have smoked it far away from camp!!).

Paulo said he wanted to 'experience it', Ishmal, as I imagined 'did not want to refuse and just went along with the crowd', Lennon thought it would give him 'a funny feeling', Aldous said he needed it 'to relax and sleep and calm down after a horrible week following his grans death', and Rocky 'wanted to share the moment with his team-mates'. I proceed to tell them about the risk they were taken to their career and endangering their ability to get signed by major football clubs.

Week 7 Fantasy football results

Name	Value	Points this week in game	Total points from all games	Current Rating out of the 22 players
Aldous	30 mill	8	65	1st
Rocky	10 mill	9	56	5th
Paulo	15 mill	7	55	4th
Lennon	5 mill	6	43	11th
Ishmal	1 mill	6	42	14th

Week 7 Fantasy class results

Name	Value	Points this week in class	Total points from all classes	Current Rating out of the 5 in class
Rocky	10 mill	9	66	1st
Paulo	15 mill	7	51	2nd
Ishmal	1 mill	7	45	3rd
Lennon	5 mill	4	28	4th
Aldous	30 mill	3	21	5th

The Beast and the buddha behaviours

I chose this moment to share another Mind-Fitness concept with the boys.

Previously I had tried to convince them that the thoughts they keep their mind focused on will create their equivalent feelings within you (positive or negative), and these new feelings will then create new behaviours from you, and then your new behaviours, will influence the behaviours of the others around you.

The 3 negative sets of thoughts (past, present and future negative) trigger our minds to activate our 'beast behavioural response', and the 3 positive sets (past, present and future positive) trigger our Minds to activate our 'buddha' behavioural response. The boys all laughed at my ridiculous words and Aldous said, 'sir WTF is our beast and buddha behaviours'?

Aldous I said, 'the buddha and the beast are just like 'David bannerman and the hulk' or 'Jekyll and hyde'. 'They both reside in you, but your 'beast' is the impulsive, thoughtless, uncontrolled stress fight or flight response of reacting to a situation which comes from an ancient and undisciplined part our mind (your Monkey-mind)'. 'Whereas your 'buddha' is your calm, controlled, intelligent, focused relaxed and confident way of responding to a situation which comes from your modern evolved higher conscious mind (your Master-mind)'.

Both the beast and the buddha mindsets generate motivational energy within us, but they feel different, the buddha energy feels confident, calm, pleasant, efficient and controlled whereas the beasts energy feels overwhelming, inefficient and uncontrollable. I reminded them of the exercise that we did, when they recalled the situations which made them perform in their best and worst game, and how recalling these different memories felt very differently inside them and the motivational energy they created felt very differently.

Furthermore, the unchannelled, uncontrolled stress levels of the beast behaviours, can make us lose a lot of energy quickly and make the body feel drained quicker in the game. I asked the boys if they have ever just 'lost it' in a game and just went berserk (they all eagerly nodded vertically and suddenly looked up more interested in the lesson), especially Lennon.

But Didn't it feel horrible and draining afterwards and did 'the beast', not generally cost you in the game (they all sheepishly groaned in agreement), especially Lennon.

Whereas the buddha response works more efficiently and its energy levels last longer and feel more pleasant. I mentioned to them that sometimes during a game, you may need to have both mindsets as you may need bursts of uncontrolled energy. However, you always want the master-mind to be controlling the beasts behaviour, as it least it will stay focused on directing and channelling the energy well. The beast response is just like imagining you have a fast sportscar and your foot is on the accelerator and so it sounds great, but you still have the handbrake on and so for all the energy and noise being generated by the car, you are not moving forward in any specific direction and using up a lot of fuel.

Remember the rule I said **'The buddha responds whereas the beast reacts'.** Now we will personalize ourselves to them, by giving a name to our buddha and our beast (there was a lot of beastly groaning at this suggestion).

These were their answers
Paulo said 'David and the hulk',
Ishmal said 'Ying and Yang'
Lennon Said 'Killer and Karma',
Aldous nonchalantly said 'Jekyll and Hyde',
Rocky said 'Hercules and Ghandi'.

Once again, I got the feeling that the boys were not convinced of this useful technique of personalising yourself and your mind to creating your behaviours, so that you can become more aware of them and communicate with them in order to control them better.

Trying to lighten the mood of boredom now in the class, I said well at least you have all made 4 new friends at camp already; your monkey-mind, your master-mind, your beast-behaviour and your buddha-behaviour (it didn't work).

Then Lennon posed a good question ' He said professor, what about boxers and UFC fighters', surely they only want the beast-behaviours? I said to the boys, 'No', have you never noticed that is the boxer who looks most confident and relaxed and controlled that usually wins the fight'.

I said, 'The great Fighters that I have worked with have all learned to train their master-mind in order to control their beast'. They all just stared blankly back at me.

To try and bring some practical relevance back to them, then I told them the story about a school I once worked in. It catered for young men with behavioural issues. They had a brilliant football team but had been expelled from every league, as they could not control their emotions and therefore their behaviours on the field.

They had learned to live mostly with their monkey minds and beast behaviours and not one coach in their earlier attachments had helped them to train their master-mind or show them how to trigger their buddha behaviours. Anyway, the saddest thing was that when I was talking to their football coach, he had told me that this school had been going for 80 years and he had seen some of the countries brightest young football talent pass through here, yet not one of those hundreds of talented boys at that school had ever made it to even a professional football team?

So I asked the boys 'why they thought that was'? Rocky said 'was it because the professional teams needed players with good temperament' I nodded and said that was partly true, but more importantly those boys could not control their monkey and master minds which meant they could not control their beast and buddha behaviours. This meant they would become a liability to any professional team, who rely on all players pulling their weight on the field. But most importantly, I told them, was that many of these boys were not good future decision-makers and could not easily commit to change, and so before they were old enough to make it to the professional game, then most of them took up very bad habits or made criminal or bad choices, which had irreversibly cost them their chance of a footballing career and cost them a place In the history of the game.

I pleaded with the 5 of them, 'don't let this be your story also boys'. But if you continue with drugs, then it may just be.

Moving forward in our life Journey?

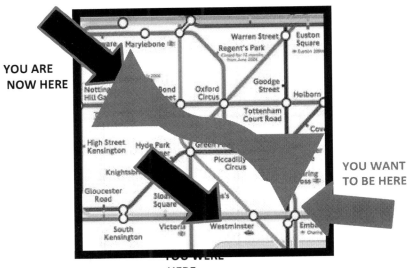

YOU ARE
NOW HERE

YOU WANT
TO BE HERE

YOU WERE
HERE

1= Definition of change commitments

Something tells me, that you have all heard the phrase 'You need to commit and start making better decisions in your game', but what does 'this' actually mean?

I told the special 5, that People do not like to admit that they have had changed their decisions, but they will be happy to say that they are willing to make new decisions based on new information they receive. Therefore, sometimes we need to feed our 'Game-mindsets', with new information, if we wish it to motivate us to create new changes in our performance.

as a mind fitness coach then these are the definitions you will learn in this class

Change commitments = Your ability that when you have a choice-moment, that you can control your impulses and decide the most helpful option to helping you reach your goal and then commit to the decision. These actions lead to an increase in our confidence, motivation, resilience and ultimately success levels.

Change-killers = Your ability that when you have a choice-moment, that you cannot control your impulses and decide on an unhelpful option which takes you further away from reaching your goal. These actions lead to a decrease in our confidence, motivation, resilience and ultimately success levels.

So you can see boys and I pointed up to the map on the wall and said

In summary so far we have discussed:

-**Awareness** is knowing where you currently are on the map and how far away that is from where you would like to be.

-**Ambition** is wanting to move forward in the future, to another desired destination.

-Goals are the travel route-plan of those specific places that you need to reach first, which lie between where you are and where your desired destination is.

-Attitude is thinking it is important enough now, to leave your current location and commit spending your focus, energy, skill and time moving on to reach your next goal.

-Focus is being able to keep your mind concentrated on staying on the correct route to your next goal.

-Motivators are the fuel which will keep you moving forward on your route to the next goal.

-Beliefs help lower **stress** and give you the **confidence** that your journey will reach the desired destination

-Change commitment starts the Physical or behavioural journey to your next goal or desired destination.

So today, I said we are going to physically start to change. I told them to all think about the one goal/ambition that they wanted to change at the start of this program and now we will create a traffic light plan for what physical commitments we need to action to achieve this goal. Traffic light plans are creating 1 thing that you would need to start doing, and 1 thing that you need to stop doing and 1 thing that you need to do more of.

Here were there answers:

PAULO
-STOP= RECALLING 1 MISTAKE
-START= REMINDING OF 1 GREAT GOAL
-MORE OF= Moving forward whenever ball is across mid-way po

-Ishmal
-STOP= focusing on what is going wrong in the game
-START= telling yourself how strong and fit you are
-MORE OF= focusing on how much time you have left

-Lennon,
-STOP= focusing on decisions by the referee
-START= telling yourself that you are needed on the pitch
-MORE OF= channeling his passion into his team-mates rather than oppoents.

-Aldous (tongue in cheek)
-STOP= always being the one who wins the game
-START= shouting more at team mates for their lack of good service
-MORE OF= winding up the opponent defenders

-Rocky
STOP= allowing myself to be distracted by the fans and not wanting to look bad in front of them
-START= being more confident and go with my first instincts
-MORE OF= taking shots and chances of my own rather than always passing to strikers

2=Why is your players ability to keep physically committing to making a change, so important in helping them perform better in the game?

So, In our inner circle of wisdom, I asked them all the question, 'Why do you think as a coach, that it is important that you help your player to get better at physically committing themself to making change improvements in their performances'?

Paulo said= So that they want to keep improving their abilities in the game

Ishmal= So that they will get better at physically keeping going even when they tired or in pain or discomfort.

Lennon= So that they can learn to give 100% in each game.

Aldous= So that they can remember the sweet taste of victory when they succeed and want to repeat it again.

Rocky= So that they learn to be proud of themselves, that even though they wanted to quit, they didn't and kept working. Even if they do not win, then they have learned resilience to keep bouncing back each time, which will keep them developing their confidence and ability.

Once again collectively they had pretty much nailed the answer.

Yes, I said 'this concept of physically committing to change, is so powerful in sports psychology and addictions, because the more we develop our ability to physically commit to changing and keep going with it, then the more we are improving our ability in the game'. This is because we are training our mind, emotions and body to work together as a team, to beat an opponent, or to get better at overcoming pain, discomfort, sacrifice, and cravings for a drug.

This team-working of the mind, emotions and body allows us to link together and give more of ourself to a performance and when we do this, we are more likely to get a result against whatever opponent we have in front of us. The victory of a result is a sweet taste, and so, we soon want more, which makes us link making changes with the 'buzz' of success.

Success makes us feel proud, but making changes also allows us to deal with the 'buzz' of not being successful, but also realizing that we have still learned and improved our game in the process. This helps to nurture our resilience and the 'buzz' of wanting to try again, because we now have more information about our opponents strengths and weaknesses, which means we can adjust our tactics, to play the opponent better and chase the 'buzz' of victory once again . Therefore whether we are successful or not, making our mind, emotions and body work together as a team, to make any change begins to improve our resilience levels (the ability to learn and keep bouncing back from change or defeat), in order to play better and improve our future game. This also helps us with our confidence levels, to do better in the next performance against the same opponent. I told them that this reminded me of the quote

'If you haven't succeeded yet, then you haven't failed enough times'

3=Where does our ability to commit to physical changes come from, or how do we nurture more commitment in our player?

So, I asked the boys the usual question 'Where do you think that we get our ability to stay committed to making physical changes in your game from"?

Paulo said= You get it from how committed your coach is about winning the game
Ishmal= You get it from thinking about how much pleasure you will get from the victory (he was starting to sound like Aldous)
Lennon= You get it from your team-mates and how committed they are to beating the opponents.
I noticed that Aldous had kept quiet and had a look of 'danger' about him.
So I went onto Rocky and he said 'Professor, 'you can get it from how competitive and motivated that you are about wanting to do yourself proud and become the best you possible, by believing that you can keep moving forward on your journey and improving towards your best potential (another bloody great answer from rocky)

Then Aldous stood up angrily and exclaimed 'You get it from your parents, and if they are committed to each other and stay committed to you, then it teaches you to stay committed in your game'. If on the other hand, they cannot keep their commitment to each other or keep their commitment to loving and nurturing you, then the chances are you will not learn how to commit to difficult changes in your game either'.
This was the second time that I had really seen a 'damaged', vulnerable, yet honest emotional side to Aldous (the first was when his gran died). For another moment, I got a glimpse of the real player that he could have been, rather than having to witness his usual fake peacock routine, strutting about proud and confident and always showing off to the crowd. I genuinely took a moment in awe of this new wonderful player before me,

this was a brief window in time, that we all got a glimpse of the world-class player that he could have been with all his natural potential.

Then I realized as I stared at him, that I had kept the awkward silence going on too long, as all the boys were now staring at me. So, I thanked Aldous for his honest contribution and agreed that yes, 'levels of commitment ability, were another gift (or curse) that parents would often pass onto their children.

It was this fallible, vulnerable and human Aldous that I witnessed in this moment, which I would always try and remember in the future, even after, I had heard of some of the terrible things he had done.

Well done, I said once again all your answers fit nicely to the question. Your ability to make and keep going with physical commitments can come from various sources including; your coaches, team-mates, thinking about the rewards of your efforts, your pride and competitiveness, and how much you believe in your potential to improve and be the best you possible. Finally, yes, your parents can help to train commitment in you, 'or not', I said as I made a side-glance towards Aldous who was now sitting quietly staring out of the window and looking a little embarrassed.

4=How do we measure if our player has the correct level of Physical change commitment before each game?

So I said 'as a coach, the important thing to remember is that your players ability to bring their mind, emotions and body together to work as team and to physically make a change begins to improve our resilience in the game, as well as our confidence to do better in the next performance'.

So my next question to all of them was '**As a coach, How would you measure if your player has a high enough level of Physical commitment before each game?**

Here were there answers:

Paulo said= You get it from the physical effort they have put into training that week

Ishmal= You ask them to commit to the rest of the team in the dressing room beforehand, that they will produce a certain level of committed performance on the game.

Lennon= You get it from asking them, how much they want to beat their opponents today

Aldous (almost instantly followed with) 'and how good it will make them feel to beat them

Rocky= Professor, you ask them if there is anything that could currently stop them being able to commit to performing their best today?

Well done, I said 'these are all ways to measure your players level of physical commitment to performing 100% in the game today'.

You get it from the physical effort they have put into their training before the game. You can get them to commit to the other team members that they are willing to give their all. You measure it from asking them how important it is for them to beat their opponents today and do they think the feelings of victory will be worth giving all of their physical commitment too.

And you can get it from asking them is there anything that could stop them committing their full mind, emotions and physical ability into playing the game today, right up until the final whistle blows.

I then told them the story of the 'Stanford university Marshmallow experiment' (they all started laughing, but stopped when they realised I was serious). Or as I said, some people now refer to it as, 'how to tell if you child is going to become an addict'.

Basically I told them ' the researchers worked with children aged 4-6 years old and they put them in a room on their own with 5 marshmallows on a table'.

Next , they told them that if they could sit in the room for 5 minutes on their own and not touch, lick or eat the marshmallows, then they would get a big bag of marshmallows as a reward when they left'.

Then the researchers left and monitored the children's behaviours on video.

The result was that those children who had already mastered the ability of master-mind and impulse control, in order to make that 5 minute commitment and not eat the marshmallows (by closing their eyes, counting, singing or sitting on their hands), when they followed up these children's life progress 30 years later, the majority had high success rates in life and low addiction rates. Whereas the children who did not have that master-mind ability and therefore gave in to their monkey-mind and could not beat the impulse and ate the marshmallows quickly, when they were followed up 30 years later, they had low success rates in life and high addiction rates.

I told the boys' this experiment is not a test of addiction, but more importantly it is a test of being able to see Future rewards (or consequences) for a present behaviour and then having the ability to control your present impulses and stick to the commitment you made, in order to gain the reward for your future self'.

5= What techniques can we use, to help to improve our players Physical commitment towards their performance in Changing to improve their game.

Technique 7: Ice-Bucket commitment

I then taught the boys a nice quick technique for improving your commitment.

I Brought in 5 buckets of ice and asked them each to state a realistic time that they would be willing to commit too keeping their hands and arms in each bucket of ice.

I asked them if they were all happy to commit to 1 minute (they agreed).

And so I played the song 'ice ice baby' by vanilla ice and timed them all doing this (they did not appreciate my musical irony).

They each managed the 1minute ice-bucket challenge and I clapped and congratulated them (they all looked very proud of themselves).

Now I told them to keep nurturing commitment in your player, then you would repeat this exercise but each time you would commit to a longer time of discomfort with your hand in the bucket. This would enable you to become more committed to being resilient against discomfort for longer and longer and this skill in life would be invaluable (recall the Stanford university marshmallow children).

The boys seemed to like these interactive techniques and they all did well at their physical commitments to the ice-bucket exercises.

Next, in order to calm them down then I told them we were going to watch a film-scene with Morgan Freeman in the 'shawshank redemption'. This scene of him going for prison parole, was a nice example about the power of sometimes not giving into impulse when your young, but rather to being able to think ahead to the future consequences, because unfortunately our future selves cannot come back and give us advice.

I then decided to share my own personal story with the boys about a time when I was young that my father caught me drinking. I thought he would really punish me, but instead he quietly told me that I would have many years in the future to drink as much as I wished.

However, seeing as I was only young just now, then I should enjoy my childhood years doing childish things, because they wouldn't last long and I couldn't get them back when they were gone, even with all the alcohol in the world.

I urged the boys 'that their future selves will have many years to do whatever they wish, after their football playing days are over, But they should focus on enjoying everything linked to football just now, because when their game is gone, all the weed in the world (even the strongest skunk) won't be able to bring it back.

I asked the boys to look up at their map again and I said 'These physical commitments to change is the equivalent of your driver now getting into the car, starting the engine and driving away from where you were before'.

I asked the boys this week if 'anyone had found the £10,000 treasure box', which the head coach Frank had hidden someone in the camp and The clue to its whereabouts was; **'The sooner that you can see the process, then the next part of the journey will unveil itself and the treasure will be found'.**

They all groaned "NO".

Then I proceeded to award them their fantasy class scores for this session and I wrote these up on the wall next to their fantasy football scores then

The boys as always moaned about their class scores and pointed out that their class results, did not mirror their football results, but as I always said to them
'Guys, there is a still a lot of time left for you to play in the game and who says that I am talking about football!.

And as they all went buzzing out of the room, with one arm dripping with ice and water, I shouted back to them **'Remember boys, 'You never lose in this game, you only win or you learn'.** They couldn't care less.

Moving forward in our life Journey?

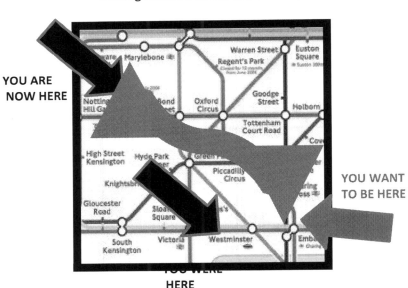

YOU ARE
NOW HERE

YOU WANT
TO BE HERE

HERE

Chapter 14= Physical Resilience versus rejection

PILARS LAW 8= *You currently are where you are in the game, based on how you have chosen to spend your Focus, Energy, skill and Time. However, all mindsets and their emotions and therefore behaviours are all fluid and changeable and so we can travel between 3 states; Previous, changing or changed.*
If change is not happening then you are not putting the amount of Focus, Energy, Skill or Time into it, which it requires.

'There is no elevator to success, but the stairs are always available'
Joe Girard

When I entered the classroom, the boys were all looking dejected and fed up. I had already heard that they had lost this week and Aldous had been knocked off top spot in the league by his twin brother. Rocky was 5th, Paulo was 8th, and lennon 12th and Ishmal 14th.

In class it was still Rocky, Paulo, Ishmal, Lennon and Aldous in that respective order.

As we sat like we did at the beginning of every lesson In our circle of strength to discuss the highs and lows of the week then I asked them all 'why the horse-like long faces'?

'We all have had a bad week', Paulo replied, 'I was dumped by the girl that I had met a few weeks ago in town and who I really liked', and I could see he was far more distressed and upset about this than he cared to let on to the other boys. I asked him 'if he wanted to talk about his feelings for the girl, or how was he coping with this love-rejection and not being able to spend time with her in a relationship anymore, but he quietly said , 'No'.

Ishmal said nothing, lennon said that 'his agent had wrote to say that his favoured club had rejected the offer to sign him', and I could see this had been a major blow to Lennon as he had his heart set on this club only. I asked Lennon, 'if he wanted to talk about how this career-rejection had affected him and did he have a plan of what other clubs may be a better fit for him?", but he murmured back 'No, he didn't feel like talking at this time'.

Aldous was annoyed at his relegation into 2nd place in the fantasy football league and Rocky said that 'he had a decent week' (much to the dismay of the others).

I pointed out to them their fantasy class league results, which probably didn't help any of them cheer up either (although I could see for the corner of my eye, Rocky having a wry smile to himself)

But in my usual upbeat tone I said ' **but don't worry boys, as there was a still a lot of time left to play in the game yet, and who said that I am talking about football.**

To my ears, this never ceased to be funny.

Week 8 Fantasy football results

Name	Value	Points this week in game	Total points from all games	Current Rating out of the 22 players
Aldous	30 mill	9	74	2nd
Rocky	10 mill	9	65	5th
Paulo	15 mill	7	62	8th
Lennon	5 mill	7	50	12th
Ishmal	1 mill	6	48	14th

Week 8 Fantasy class results

Name	Value	Points this week in class	Total points from all classes	Current Rating out of the 5 in class
Rocky	10 mill	9	75	1st
Paulo	15 mill	7	58	2nd
Ishmal	1 mill	7	52	3rd
Lennon	5 mill	4	32	4th
Aldous	30 mill	3	24	5th

1= Definition of Resilience versus submission

Something tells me, that you have all heard the phrase 'No pain, no gain or you don't see results straight away, or you need perseverance or willpower in this game', but what does 'these phrases' actually mean?

This week in your certificate course called '**so you think you could be a coach**', we will be discussing resilience and its opposing skill 'submission' and how you nurture resilience within your player.

I told the special 5, that 'People often prefer to use phrases like 'willpower' as a way of describing some kind of genetic trait that your either born with or your not, rather than admit that resilience and keeping going, is something which we can all train within us'.

I guess it easier I said, 'in this modern world, to blame a lack of skill in playing the game on a 'genetic trait' (I was just born without willpower), rather than admit your lack of skill, may come from a lack of good coaching or a lack of actually spending time learning what the rules of the game are, or a lack of time and effort spent on nurturing your skills in playing the game'.

With a feeling of self-pride, I then told them the famous Scottish story of 'Robert the Bruce' and the spider and how this spider's actions to not give up spinning its web, inspired his own resilience levels, and he went on to conquer England afterwards. They sneered and shouted out that I was being racist with this story, so I quickly changed topic.

I said to them, 'The phrase 'resilience' for the purpose of this class is your ability to keep actively repeating, but improving the process of making a change despite a lack of visible results at this time.

Resilience= This is your ability to keep actively repeating whilst improving the process of making a change despite a lack of visible results at this time.

These actions lead to an increase in our learning, hope, belief, experience, knowledge and skills in the game.

Submission = This is your ability to give up physically repeating a process of making change due to a lack of visible results at this time.
These actions lead to a decrease in our confidence, motivation, resilience and ultimately success levels. And an increase in our laziness, cynicism, regret, resentment, regret

So you can see boys and I pointed up again to the map on the wall
-**Awareness** is knowing where you currently are on the map and how far away that is from where you would like to be.
-**Ambition** is wanting to move forward in the future, to another desired destination.
-**Goals** are the travel route-plan of those specific places that you need to reach first, which lie between where you are and where your desired destination is.
-**Attitude** is thinking it is important enough now, to leave your current location and commit spending your focus, energy, skill and time moving on to reach your next goal .
-**Focus** is being able to keep your mind concentrated on staying on the correct route to your next goal.

-**Motivators** are the fuel which will keep you moving forward on your route to the next goal.

-**Beliefs** give you the **confidence** that your journey will reach the desired destination.

-**Change commitment** starts the Physical journey to the next goal'.

But I said **Resilience**, is the ability that helps you to keep getting out in the rain to fix a flat tyre, whenever you get one, and then get back in your car to carry on with the physical journey to your desired destination.

I then told them the story about the tennis player that I had worked with, who had a weak back-hand, and this always frustrated and annoyed him. So, he tended to try and not play the shot now during his matches, as he was worried that this shot would lose him the point. He had now trained himself to avoid the shot as he disliked it so much, that this was now costing him matches, as he was choosing other easier shots to play instead. However, these easier shots, were often not the best decisions. We worked on getting his mind and his emotions and his body to start working as a team to enjoy (rather than get frustrated) at the challenge of repeating the shot and of tasting the victory of seeing any small improvements In his shot.

He used the sensory alarm technique that I have shown you, to keep reminding him to use his mind and emotions to focus on enjoying the improvement journey rather than just think about the quality of the end-shot or destination. For 2 weeks solid, he kept repeating hitting a ball back and forth off a wall but enjoying it, and by the end he was celebrating the victory of hitting a very good backhand the majority of the times. He went to have his best season ever that year.

2=Why is your players ability to be resilient and keep actively repeat and improve the process of making a change, so important in helping them perform better in the game?

So, In our inner circle of wisdom, I asked them all the question, 'Why do you think as a coach, that it is so important that you help your player to get better at being resilient and to keep actively repeat and improve the process of making a change'?

Paulo said= 'So that they keep improving their abilities in the game'.
Ishmal= 'So that they will understand how important it is for them to keep going even when they are tired or in pain or discomfort'.
Lennon= 'So that they can learn to give 110% in each game' (this boy needed a math's lesson).
Aldous = 'So that they can keep repeating being successful and keep repeating the sweet taste of always winning each game'.
Rocky= So that they learn the process of learning and enjoy reflecting on what went wrong and what went well and to be proud of themselves, that even though they may have wanted to quit, as the result was not going their way, they didn't and they kept playing. Even if they do not win, then they have learned the resilience to keep bouncing back each time, which will keep them developing their confidence and ability and belief that victory is coming.

Once again, funnily enough they had collectively nailed the answer.

Yes, I said 'this concept of repeating the art of actively committing to change, is so powerful in sports psychology and addictions, because the more we develop our ability to actively commit to change and keep repeating it, then the more we are learning to improve our ability in each game that we play every day. It develops in us the power of self-critical reflection, which requires your awareness and honesty, but really helps you to focus on ways to improve your game for tomorrow. That way you know your game will always move forward no matter what position you may find yourself having to play in the future. Reflection and improved repetition are the hallmarks of what has made all great players what they are today, but these skills also require the resilience to keep getting back up on that horse and learning how to do better next time.

3=Where does our resilience to keep actively repeating and learning physical changes come from?

So, I asked the boys, 'where do you think that our resilience levels to keep actively repeating and learning physical changes come from'?

Paulo said (wait for it, drum-roll)= 'They get it from their training by the coach'.
Ishmal= 'They get it from thinking about how much it could improve their chance of becoming a professional player'.
Lennon= 'They get it from how resilient their team-mates are'.
Aldous= 'They get it from believing they are the best player EVER, and want to show everyone else they are the best by earning the most amount of money and medals in the game'. (well, at least he wasn't blaming his parents this time for his levels of resilience, although ironically I would have accepted this as an answer).
Rocky said 'Professor, they can get it from their value of self-worth and belief in themselves that they can reach their potential'.

Well done, I said once again all your answers fit nicely to the question.

'Your ability to improve your levels of resilience to keep actively repeating and improving your physical abilities in the game, can come from various sources including; your coaches, team-mates, thinking about the rewards of your repetition, your pride and competitiveness, and how much you believe in your potential to improve and be your best player possible. Finally, although you all missed it this time, yes your parents can also help to train resilience In you, 'or not', I said as I scowled over at Aldous, who had now fell asleep, probably due to a lack of genetics.

4=How do we measure if our player has the correct level of resilience before each game?

So as a coach, the important thing to remember is that your players (and teams) ability to be resilient during a game, will enable them to adapt quicker and better to any unforeseen problems which may arise, without the need for anger and frustration, which can often

cost a team, the loss of a few players due to ill-discipline. I told them, that I had personal experience of losing a game to this issue.

They all laughed judgingly at me and said 'Professor, we didn't even know that you had ever been a player' in the game.

I ignored their derisory sneers and continued by saying, 'increasing the players (and teams) resilience levels, will also help improve their ability to successfully change tactics at half-time, if the opponent is winning and a **change is needed** to improve their chance of getting victory in the game.

So my next question to all of them became '**As a coach, How do you measure if your player has a high level of resilience before each game?**

Here were there answers:

Paulo said= 'You get it from the physical effort they have put into training that week ',(this was his answer to everything).

Ishmal= 'You ask them what they are going to change, if the person they are marking in the game, is getting the better of them'?

Lennon= 'You get it from asking them how much they have learned about their opponents strengths and weaknesses today'.

Aldous= 'you get it from how much is it worth for them to beat their opponents today and taste victory'.

Rocky= 'Professor, you ask them if there is anything that they hope to improve upon and learn today from their performance'.

Well done, I said 'these are all ways to measure your players level of resilience before the game.

You get it from the physical effort they have put into their training before the game. You can get it from how many other strategies and improvements that they have available to use against their opponent, if things are not going well with their first tactics. You get it from their level of thought and planning about their opponents strengths and weaknesses and therefore which tactics that would work well against these. You get it from how much victory is worth it to them in this game, as this will be a measure of how much they are willing to keep coming back and fighting against their opponent until the final whistle blows. Finally, you get it from knowing what they hope to learn and improve about their game during this performance and the level of reflection they put in afterwards

5= What techniques can we use, to help to improve our players resilience repetition levels towards their performance in Changing to improve their game.

Technique 8: Boxing bag 3 rounds challenge
I then taught them a simple technique for repeating a challenge even if it is getting harder.
I took them through to the gym area, where there were 5 boxing bags. I asked them all to put on gloves and what they need to do was to now keep punching the bags non-stop for three rounds of 3 minutes. Each round would get harder than the last, but this is where they would use the mind-set techniques that we had previously worked on to ensure they began to focus on self-talk and thoughts which were helpful to their resilience, determination and motivation, to help them keep going even though the discomfort would be increasing.
This was the most difficult task I had set them so far, but I felt they all had enough Mind-Fitness techniques now to cope. I played the song from the Rocky film, **eye of the Tiger by Survivor,** to see if it would help motivate them.

Nine minutes later, they were groaning in relief of pain when my stopwatch ended their ordeal. I was very proud to see that they all did it, even though it was extremely tough on them all (some more than others).
I asked them how they felt about themselves now, and I could see they were all proud of their achievement against 9 minutes of discomfort. I asked them to remember what they were focusing on which had helped them to keep going and to remember these resilient-thoughts when playing in the game on Sunday.

I ended this session by saying to the boys that we all experience rejection in life, but it is those that can reflect on it, and learn about how they can improve their performance next time , so that each time they repeat and reflect they get better and closer to defeating whichever opponent is in their game.

I Turned to Paulo and said there will be other girls who may you reject you in your life, but you just need to work out how you can keep becoming a better boyfriend each time.

Lennon there will be other job rejections, but you just need to keep reflecting on becoming a better player for any club.

And Aldous, there will be times that people score more than us, but we just need to keep working out how we can improve on scoring our goals.

I turned to them all and told them the story that the famous boxer Muhammed Ali once said 'that he never counted the number of sit-ups he did, he only started counting when it started hurting, because the only important number was the amount of these ones that he did'.

This boxer was also famous for his quote; **'Your only a failure when you stop trying'.**

I asked the boys to look up at their map again and I said 'These resilience repetitions are the equivalent of being able to get your driver out of car in the rain when you get a flat tyre and to keep fixing these flat tyres until you are moving forward again to your next desired destination.

I asked the boys this week if 'anyone had found the £10,000 treasure box', which the head coach Frank had hidden someone in the camp and The clue to its whereabouts was;
'The sooner that you can see the process, then the next part of the journey will unveil itself and the treasure will be found'.

They all groaned as ever "NO".

Then I proceeded to award them their fantasy class scores for this session and I wrote these up on the wall next to their fantasy football scores then

The boys as always moaned about their class scores and pointed out that their class results, did not mirror their football results, but as I always said to them
'Guys, there is a still a lot of time left for you to play in the game and who says that I am talking about football!.

And as they all went limping out of the room with sore arms, I hailed back to them '**Remember boys, 'You never lose in this game, you only win or you learn'.**
They had already disappeared.

Moving forward in our life Journey?

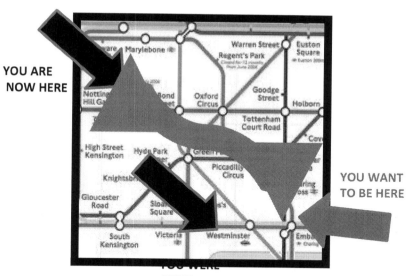

Week 8 Fantasy football results

Name	Value	Points this week in game	Total points from all games	Current Rating out of the 22 players
Aldous	30 mill	9	74	2nd
Rocky	10 mill	9	65	5th
Paulo	15 mill	7	62	8th
Lennon	5 mill	7	50	12th
Ishmal	1 mill	6	48	14th

Week 8 Fantasy class results

Name	Value	Points this week in class	Total points from all classes	Current Rating out of the 5 in class
Rocky	10 mill	9	75	1st
Paulo	15 mill	7	58	2nd
Ishmal	1 mill	7	52	3rd
Lennon	5 mill	4	32	4th
Aldous	30 mill	3	24	5th

Chapter 15= Results versus reversors

Physical PILARS LAW 9= *Why we Change and what helps us keep changing is based on the 4E's. The 4E's state that change needs to make life more; Easier, Enjoyable, Effective or Equal for us, or we will give up on it.*

'It's better to create something others criticise, then to create nothing and criticise others
-Ricky Gervais

When I entered the classroom, the boys were all squawking away that I couldn't make out what they were saying.

Finally, when I managed to get them to calm down, I asked what they were all so animated about. Lennon eventually told me that 'Aldous had decided to quit and leave us, he was going to leave the class and the summer-camp'.

I asked the boys if they wanted to sit down in our circle of trust and Aldous could explain his decision for us.

Aldous sat bored and frustrated looking, and said that he felt he was neither getting any results in this class nor any better at football at the summer-camp, so it was better just to quit now.

Incidentally, I had heard in the coaches staffroom this morning that for the second week in a row the boys team had lost and Aldous was sitting now at no.3 spot in the fantasy football league behind his twin brother and a boy from Liverpool. I asked the boys one by one in a clockwise manner, if they would like to respond to Aldous's decision by telling him how they felt about him leaving the team.

Paulo had said 'that he felt Aldous had decided too quickly and he should just give it 1 more week before deciding, and then he would respect whatever decision Aldous made then'.

Ishmal seemed the most worried about Aldous leaving and told Aldous, 'that he had helped him a lot at this camp with his confidence and that he didn't know if he could manage to get to the end of the camp without Aldous being here in his team', (Aldous never reacted).

Lennon seemed the most upset at Aldous's decision and said 'that he would miss Aldous a lot as he really enjoyed his company and he had helped make the summer-camp, a lot more fun and a lot more cool place to spend time in', (Aldous never reacted).

Rocky said that 'he thought Aldous was too good a player to give up on his team-mates, as they would be a far weaker team without him, and that if he stayed to the end he would probably win the summer-camp trophy and get signed up by a great premiership team', (Aldous never reacted)..

I looked over at Aldous and he didn't seem too bothered about the heartfelt words that his teammates had offered him, about their feelings towards him leaving. I wondered at that point if Aldous was just going to be one of those players that would always leave his teammates, when he wasn't winning anymore. Or was it simply because his team had lost twice in a row and he hadn't been at the top of the fantasy football league for the last 2 weeks and he now genuinely feared not winning the summer-camp trophy. I imagined that he would rather quit feeling safe, yet blind in the 'not knowing', rather than stay and fight and find out the truth, if he was the best or not.

It was at this point that I knew that Aldous would never make it to his full potential, in the big cruel professional game.

As a distraction, I asked what they thought about losing again twice in a row. They all gruntled something about 'we were robbed', but I could tell by their 'protestations' that they were half-hearted. Their fantasy football league positions were as follows Aldous 3rd, Rocky was 5th, Paulo was 9th, Lennon 13th, and Ishmal 15th.

In class it was still Rocky, Paulo, Ishmal, Lennon and Aldous in that respective order.

But in a less than usual upbeat tone I said '**don't worry boys, as there is a still a lot of time left to play in the game yet, and who said that I am talking about football**'.
But even I was getting fed up of this mantra now.

Okay I said this week in your certificate course '**So you think you could be a coach**', then we are going to discuss results versus reversors (I glanced over at Aldous, but he never seemed to get the connection).

Week 9 Fantasy football results

Name	Value	Points this week in game	Total points from all games	Current Rating out of the 22 players
Aldous	30 mill	9	83	3rd
Rocky	10 mill	8	73	5th
Paulo	15 mill	7	69	9th
Lennon	5 mill	7	57	13th
Ishmal	1 mill	6	54	15th

Week 9 Fantasy class results

Name	Value	Points this week in class	Total points from all classes	Current Rating out of the 5 in class
Rocky	10 mill	9	84	1st
Paulo	15 mill	8	66	2nd
Ishmal	1 mill	7	59	3rd
Lennon	5 mill	4	36	4th
Aldous	30 mill	3	27	5th

1= Definition of Results versus Reversors

Something tells me, that you have all heard the phrase 'When I start getting results then I will put more effort in' or 'what's the point of keeping going as I don't feel that I am getting any results, in fact I am getting worse'.

I told the special 5, that 'People often make the mistake of saying they will only really put a lot of effort into something, once they have seen some results first'. This is a strange game-mindset I said, because it's the equivalent of saying that you are only willing to put effort into playing your game, if the referee can guarantee you beforehand, that you are going to win.

I told the boys the story of a client I worked with years ago who said 'that she was only willing to start exercising and eating healthy once the universe had made her experience how it felt to be her desired target weight first'. I imagine that the woman is still out there praying to the universe for some divine nutrition.

I said to them, 'The phrase 'results' and is opposing skill 'reversors or relapses', for the purpose of this mind fitness class, are defined below and I wrote these on the class board.

Results = Your ability to continue with momentum in the change process because you have seen or experienced positive outcomes from your efforts of actively repeating a change process. These actions lead to an increase in our confidence, happiness, motivation, ambition and belief,

Reversors or relapses= Your ability to reverse back to a previous behaviour or mindset, despite having seen or experienced positive outcomes from your efforts of actively repeating a change process. These actions lead to a decrease in our confidence, motivation, ambition, resilience and ultimately success levels and an increase in our laziness, cynicism, regret, resentment, guilt, shame and regret.

I then made a very Scottish joke, that in Scotland a 'short relapse' in behavior is just called a 'wee-lapse' rather than a 'relapse'. Not surprisingly, this Scottish dialect humour of mine flew way past them and they all looked at me like I was some kind of loser.

Anyway, quickly moving on, 'So you can see boys that so far we have covered, as I pointed up again to the map on the wall

-Awareness is knowing where you currently are on the map and how far away that is from where you would like to be.

-Ambition is wanting to move forward in the future, to another desired destination.

-Goals are the travel route-plan of those specific places that you need to reach first, which lie between where you are and where your desired destination is.

-Attitude is thinking it is important enough now, to leave your current location and commit spending your focus, energy, skill and time moving on to reach your next goal .

-Focus is being able to keep your mind concentrated on staying on the correct route to your next goal.

-Motivators are the fuel which will keep you moving forward on your route to the next goal.

-Beliefs give you the **confidence** that your journey will reach the desired destination

-Change commitment starts the Physical journey to the next goal'

-Resilience helps you to keep getting out in the rain to fix a flat tyre, whenever you get one, and then get back in your car to carry on with the physical journey to your desired destination.

This week, we will consider results to be the equivalent of watching the photo and video highlights of all the beautiful scenery and amazing landmarks that you have already seen on the journey so far. These photos and videos, help us to keep physically want to keep going on further on our journey, to see what even more amazing things we may find at the next desired destination.

So today, I said we are going to help you to use your results that you have received so far in your game since week 1 to help keep building the momentum for you to keep changing in the last 3-4 weeks of summer camp.

I told them to all think about at least one result that they have gained from the start of summer camp, and today we are going to enjoy wallowing in our own self-success.

I thought Aldous would especially like this, but he didn't seem that excited.

2=Why is your players ability to be aware and focus on their personal results from a change process, so important in helping them to keep performing better in the game?

So, In our inner circle of wisdom, I asked the boys the question, 'Why do you think as a coach, that it is so important for you to help your player become more aware of the personal results and improvements that they have gained from actively undertaking a change in their game performance'?

Paulo said= 'So that they can enjoy knowing that they have developed and got better in the game'.

Ishmal= 'So that they increase their confidence levels in their own abilities'.

Lennon= 'So that they can appreciate that it is their work and effort which have made them a better player'.

Aldous= 'So that they want to keep getting the 'buzz' of getting more results'.

Rocky= 'So that they see the benefits of the process of actively learning and improvement changing'.

Once again no surprises, they had collectively pretty much nailed the answer.

Yes, I said this 'concept of being aware of how far you have travelled in the game so far, by focusing on the results which you have gained by actively trying to change and improve your game performance, is so powerful in sports psychology'. The more we develop our desire to enjoy the results of change, the more confidence we gain in ourselves and this increases our ambition to desire more change (change begets change).

Reminiscing about results help us to appreciate that the improvement process does require work, but that if we see and feel the benefits as worth it, then change can be a real 'buzz'. If we don't have these results, then the journey starts to seem long and arduous and unrewarding and we begin to think of giving up and just heading back to where we originally came from.

I then told them about this golfer that I had worked with, who had just completed his first couple of years on the European Pro Tour. He had been a fine amateur who had won many prestigious tournaments, but all of a sudden this year he had not even been in the top 10 in any of his tournaments and he had failed to make 'the cut' in most of the pro-tournaments he had entered. This change from winning amateur to 'losing professional, had really affected his confidence and desire and love of competing in the game. He was ready to give up after 1 year in the professional ranks, until I had pointed out that his personal results were improving with each round of the European tour that he had played. We then worked out that if he kept developing at this rate then within 2 years, he would win his first competition. We programmed a few alarm-sensor techniques to keep reminding him of these improvements. Needless to say, he won the first of his 8 European tournaments 2 years later.

3=Where does our ability to be able to stop and remind ourselves of the results and highlights of our journey so far come from?

So, I asked the circle of boys, 'where do you think that a player's ability to be able to routinely remind themselves of the results and highlights of their journey in the game so far, comes from?

Paulo said= 'They get it from their coach' (come on, what else would he say).

Ishmal= 'They get it from setting up 'alarm-sensors' which will periodically remind them of achievements or highlights from their journey' (at least this boy had finally been listening to me).

Lennon= 'They get it from their team-mates reminding them of the great results they have had', (this boy had obviously experienced different dressing-room environments than I had). As, normally your team-mates who are young insecure males (even when they are adults), would only take pleasure in recalling your worst embarrassing moments in these situations!!

Aldous= 'They get it from having to repeat telling themselves that they are really good and talented and deserve to win the game', (Wait for it,) 'because if they don't tell themselves this, then they will be told constantly by their parents that they are still not performing good enough or nothing they do will ever be good enough, as they always know someone else's son, who has done better in the game'. It was obvious now, that Aldous had real issues with his parents and if he left these unresolved and did not seek help for them, then I was certain these would be part of his future downfall.

Rocky said 'Professor, they could get it from routinely watching the videos of some of their best performances, and Spending time reminiscing over the medals and trophies that they have won to date. These tactics would help remind them, of what they have previously enjoyed and achieved in the game, whilst making them aware that they are still capable of going even further in the game.

Well done, I said once again all your answers fit nicely to the question. Your ability to be good at reminding yourselves of your results and highlights of your journey so far, can be developed by your coaches (I nodded to Paulo), or your team-mates (I sarcastically frowned at Lennon), or from deliberately setting up alarm-sensors (I beamed a proud smile at Ishmal)
Or from learning self-praise through self-meditation or alternatively, just wanting to prove your parents wrong (I glanced at Aldous, knowing that he would avert his eyes).
Finally, we can get it from Reminiscing over past video highlights of the success we have already experienced in the game from all of our hard work and effort on our journey so far (I pointed over to Lennon)

4=How do we measure if our player has the correct level of results-reminiscence before each game?

So, as a coach, the important thing to remember is that your players (and teams) ability to remind themselves of past successes and glories (results-reminiscence) will help enable them to play with ambition, enjoyment, confidence, belief, and resilience. As you remind them
of their moments of resilience which helped them snatched victory before, then this will breed more resilience and desire for more results in them as a collective team. If you cannot do this, then they will give up their fight, quicker in the game.

So my next question to all of them became 'As a coach, How do you measure if your player has a high level of results-reminiscence before each game?
Here were there answers:

Paulo said= 'You ask them what their personal best performance in a game has been'.
Ishmal= 'You ask them what their best team result has been.
Lennon= 'You get it from asking them what tactics they think would be good in this game, as they have worked previously with similar opponents'.

Aldous = 'You get it from asking them to predict the score today based on previous games with similar opponents'.

Rocky= 'Professor, you ask them what is their favourite memory of them or the team being able to turn a game around, and how they think that they managed to do this'.

Well done, I said 'these are all ways to measure your players level of 'results-reminiscence' before each game. You get it from asking them before a new game about their previous favourite personal and team performances. You get it from asking them what tactics they think would work based on previous tactics that went well. You can enhance it by getting them to predict the score of this performance based on previous similar opponents and finally you get it from asking them to recall times when they resiliently snatched victory from the jaws of defeat.

5= What techniques can we use, to help to improve our players results-reminiscence.

Technique 9: Watching Game Highlights in your relaxation room with progressive muscle relaxation.
In order to enjoy time reminiscing over results. I asked the boys to close their eyes and imagine that they could design their own house in their mind, with loads of different rooms that would have the ability to make them feel different if they were inside of them. For instance a swimming pool and shower room that could energise them, a gym that could make them feel stronger, a bedroom for when they need to rest, a music room to uplift them, or a games room where they could escape reality or go and watch TV and relax.
Now in this fantasy house in their mind, I wanted them now to go to their 'games chilling room' with a big tv screen and massage chair. I then asked them to get out their mindfulness mask as we would be practicing our mindfulness breathing

again, but this time we would also add in a progressive muscle relaxation exercise.

I got them to put on their mindfulness mask and then to close their eyes and start to breathe (smell the flowers and then blow out the birthday candles). To help with the relaxation Then I played them the song 'relax' by frankie goes to Hollywood (this turned out to be a big mistake and a schoolboy error on my part), as they never took the exercise as seriously as I would have wanted. But, I asked them to tense up the muscles in their eyes and forehead until it became a little uncomfortable, at which point they would release these muscles and breath out, whilst pinching their motivational point and seeing one of their great past results appear on the TV screen in their games-chilling room.

We then repeated cycles of this for different parts of the body (neck, shoulders, arms, hands, stomach, legs, feet and toes).

When they finally completed this exercise of relaxing whilst watching the highlights of their game so far on the screen and opened their eyes, then I could see that they all seemed more relaxed, proud and confident in themself and their game so far. Whilst looking more determined to keep going further and achieve more in their game.

They all enjoyed the experience of being in their minds-room and watching highlight results of their game so far.

I told the boys this technique works because it links the pleasure of imagining watching your game highlights at the same time that your breathing is relaxing and your muscles are becoming more relaxed in your body. Finally, we link both these pleasant cognitive and physical feelings together by creating a motivational pinch which programs your brain to remember these highlight results of your game and to feel relaxed when it does.

Their homework was to repeat this blended technique of mind-room with progressive relaxation with motivational pinching each night before they went to bed.

Next, I brought a TV into the class and I told the boys that we were now going to start watching videos of players taking different penalty kicks which had taken place from various football games across the world. I also played 'walk this way', by Run DMC as I stopped each video before the footballer had even struck the ball and I asked each of the boys to predict whether he thought the footballer would score the penalty or not. After 10 different videos, then they had all accurately predicted whether the footballer scored or not?

So, I asked them how they knew? 'they all answered that in each failed penalty, they could tell by the body posture, and muscle tension and the facial expressions of fear and doubt in the player, that they would not hit the ball on target and score their goal.

I agreed with them and then I said' 'wouldn't you agree boys, it was the thoughts that these players were focused on and telling themselves in their own mind, which created their change in emotions and therefore the external tension in their muscles, body and face, which you easily saw and knew would stop them scoring their goal. That is why it is so important to master your mind, because the quality of your thoughts will ultimately influence your performance to score goals. Just like it did with these penalty-takers.

For the first time in class, when I looked at them, I actually think they were beginning to take this mind-fitness stuff a bit more seriously.

I ended this session by saying to the boys In the circle. We all have times in the game when we are at low-energy and we think what is the point in carrying on, I may as well just quit or relapse and go back to where I came from. But these are the precise moments when you need to use your master-mind to go back into your super-6 set of thoughts and spend time in group number 2, called the **past positive**s where you reminisce about your results. Or if you remember **'Aldous-mode'** as we had previously called it (Aldous did not find this funny).

This technique will be useful in helping you pick your energy levels up by reminiscing on all your past results, glories success and achievements. These will re-fuel your belief and confidence and motivation in you and your resilience to pick yourself and keep moving forwards again in the game.

I said sincerely, 'boys we all relapse at some point and go backwards in the game and that is fine for a while, but reminiscing on results will give us the energy to not quit and eventually take-off forward again to the next desired destination'. 'If we do not do this and allow ourselves to wallow in our own self-pity of the relapse, then we may never move forward in the game again'. I looked over at Aldous and asked him 'to recall how many games he has been the hero and came to the rescue of his team to help them win in the dying minutes of the game'. I could see he was enjoying spending time in this set of thoughts, I genuinely hope you change your mind Aldous about leaving us, because you have a lot more game still in you and a lot of game still to learn.

He turned and winked at the other boys and said 'okay you have me for a few more weeks yet, to help you losers try and beat team B'.

I asked the boys to look up at the map on the wall again and I summarized by saying

This week we discussed why it is important on focusing on your results, on the map these are the equivalent of watching photo and video highlights of all the beautiful scenery and amazing landmarks that you have already seen on the journey so far. These photos and videos, help us to keep physically want to keep going on further on our journey, to see what amazing things we may find at the next desired destination.

I then asked the boys again this week if 'anyone had found the £10,000 treasure box', which the head coach Frank had hidden someone in the camp and The clue to its whereabouts was;
'The sooner that you can see the process, then the next part of the journey will unveil itself and the treasure will be found'.

They all groaned as ever "NO".

Then I proceeded to award them their fantasy class scores for this session and I wrote these up on the wall next to their fantasy football scores then

The boys as always moaned about their class scores and pointed out that their class results, did not mirror their football results, but as I always said to them

'Guys, there is a still a lot of time left for you to play in the game and who says that I am talking about football!.

And as they all went flying out of the room, I reminded them **'Remember boys, 'You never lose in this game, you only win or you learn'.**

They had already flew away.

Week 9 Fantasy football results

Name	Value	Points this week in game	Total points from all games	Current Rating out of the 22 players
Aldous	30 mill	9	83	3rd
Rocky	10 mill	8	73	5th
Paulo	15 mill	7	69	9th
Lennon	5 mill	7	57	13th
Ishmal	1 mill	6	54	15th

Week 9 Fantasy class results

Name	Value	Points this week in class	Total points from all classes	Current Rating out of the 5 in class
Rocky	10 mill	9	84	1st
Paulo	15 mill	8	66	2nd
Ishmal	1 mill	7	59	3rd
Lennon	5 mill	4	36	4th
Aldous	30 mill	3	27	5th

Chapter 16= Social bucket changes versus secret results

PILARS LAW 10= *We are more influenced from other people's stories and experiences than actual facts. We then control our decisions based more on other people's stories than actual facts.*

The way a team plays as a whole determines its success
 Babe Ruth

When I entered the classroom on Monday morning, the boys were all looking a bit Physically bruised (Paulo and Aldous), some had black eyes (lennon and Ishmal) and Rocky had a large cut on his forehead. I quipped and said 'was it tough game at the weekend then lads'.

But, I already knew why they were all so beaten and bruised and it wasn't from football. Once again to their utter satisfaction of the other coaches, they had informed me that my '5 special boys', had been involved in a gang punch-up in town on Saturday.

I then had to endure the usual mind-jokes from the other coaches, like, 'I thought you were teaching them how to use their minds as weapons and not their fists', and they all laughed. Although when I pointed out that I was now 2nd top of their fantasy football league table and only 1 point behind Frank, then they stopped laughing. I could see that the idea, of a sports mind-fitness academic, being able to predict better football players and teams than them, was embarrassing and bruising to their sports-ego.

Incidentally, the boys team A had won with the biggest scoreline yet at the weekend and Aldous had scored a hat-trick and was back on top of the fantasy football league. Rocky was now in 4th position, Paulo 7th, Lennon 10th and Ishmal 12th out of the 22 players at camp. Their class results were still Rocky, Paulo, Ishmal, Lennon and then Aldous.

So when I looked around the circle at these battered and bruised teenagers, I asked them in a clockwise manner to 'tell me in their words what happened, and what was their role in the event, and how did they feel about it afterwards'.

Paulo said, 'a gang of local lads came up to us, as we were sitting outside the café talking to girls. They tried to wind us up in front of the girls, saying that we were all 'nonces', as we all slept together at a posh summer camp'. Then Paulo continued 'My role was I jumped in to stop someone kicking Aldous in the head and afterwards I felt proud of myself for helping a team mate'. 'Fair enough', I replied (to Paulo's astonishment).

Ishmal told the same story, but added in that 'they called him a 'paki' and that's why Lennon punched one of them'. His role was he tried to stop the fight but got punched in the eye, and then he lost it and threw a chair at one of them. I couldn't stop a small smile escaping from my lips as I was visualising 'anxious ishmal', getting mad and launching a chair at someone in public. He said he 'felt shamed afterwards as the chair actually hit a woman sitting nearby' (the boys and me all erupted in laughter).

Lennon, told the same story, but with a sense of pride at his role in 'punching the first boy and basically starting the whole fight'. He said 'he was annoyed at allowing one of them to give him a black-eye, but he felt justified afterwards at starting the fight because of the racist remarks from the boys' (I gave him a look that said, we will discuss this later Lennon).

Aldous backed up the others story but added that he 'had 'taken two of the boys out', before a third one attacked him and kicked him from behind, and that is why he need the help of

Paulo'. His role was that he got involved 'straight after Lennon threw the first punch, in order to help his team-mate Lennon'. He also felt proud, as it made them look good in front of the girls (all the other boys agreed with this).

Finally Rocky, told the same story, he got involved after 'Ishmal had been punched in the eye and he managed to exact revenge on the guy who did it, and then another guy before one of them (not Ishmal) threw a chair at his head and cut him all the way across it'.

He said he 'also felt that his actions to help his team-mates were justified under the circumstances'.

Okay, 'fair enough', I said, Well in today's session of the certificate course '**so you think you could be a coach**', then luckily enough we will be talking about, 'The power of good teams or positive helpful social circles in helping you to develop your game'.

I told the boys' that the first 3 sessions of the certificate course were about trying to get your players mind to think differently about change, the next 3 sessions were about trying to get your player to control their emotional response to change, the last 3 sessions were getting your player to physically starting making change by themself and these final 3 sessions will about helping your player socially change their behaviours.

I said, 'This will involve discussing lobster syndrome and river otter syndrome', but the boys just looked at me, like I had finally gone mad.

1= Definition of Social bucket

I pointed up to the map on the wall and said to the boys, so far we have covered':

-**Awareness** is knowing where you currently are on the map and how far away that is from where you would like to be.

-**Ambition** is wanting to move forward in the future, to another desired destination.

-Goals are the travel route-plan of those specific places that you need to reach first, which lie between where you are and where your desired destination is.

-**Attitude** is thinking it is important enough now, to leave your current location and commit spending your focus, energy, skill and time moving on to reach your next goal .

-**Focus** is being able to keep your mind concentrated on staying on the correct route to your next goal.

-**Emotional Motivators** are the fuel which will keep you moving forward on your route to the next goal.

-Beliefs give you the confidence that your journey will reach the desired destination

-**Physical Change commitment** starts the Physical journey to the next goal'

-**Physical Resilience** helps you to keep getting out in the rain to fix a flat tyre, whenever you get one, and then get back in your car to carry on with the physical journey to your desired destination.

-**Physical Results** are like watching the video highlights of all the beautiful scenery and amazing landmarks that you have already seen on the journey now, and they help us to keep physically want to keep going on further, to see what amazing things we may find at the next goal destination

Social buckets= These are the people that you have with you in the car or on the bus with you, as you travel towards your desired destinations.

I said to the boys, Something tells me, that you have all heard the phrase 'you better start hanging around in better circles', or 'you need to find a better team to play in'.

But why do parents and coaches say that to you?

It is because real long-term change has to eventually become social change, where your attitude or behavior is changed in the social world with others (not just in the house on your own). And it usually involves having to change some of your social connections in order to get or maintain the change (i.e. gaining some new helpful social connections or losing some unhelpful connections).

I told the boys, 'that there had been some research that showed that in most cases you could predict a person's level of income, size of their house, type of car they drove, their relationship status, how many children they had, and their level of success and happiness'.

How was this done?

'by working out the average value in each category, of the 7 other adults that they spent most time with'. Their level would be the average of those 7 people. For example, the size of their house would be the average of the 7 others, and their income would be the average of the 7 other people they spent most time with (their social bucket).

Lobster and River Otter syndrome

I then told the boys, that in the addictions world, one of the most common ways of predicting if a client will return to their addiction is referred to as lobster syndrome. It is named because of the phenomena, that when fisherman capture Lobsters and bring them back to shore, then they place them in large buckets with each other and not one of the lobsters ever manage to escape.

I asked the boys, 'why do you think that none of the lobsters ever manage to escape'?

Rocky said , 'is it because they are happy being in there with one another;

'No I said, in fact they all have the desire to get out and are all trying to get out of the bucket'.

Paulo said 'is it because they do not have the ability to climb out the bucket

'No, I said, in fact not only do they have the desire to get out, but lobsters also have the ability to climb out of the bucket'.

I looked over, but the other 3 just stared gormlessly back at me. So, I said 'the final chance to get it right, I will repeat the clues once again, 'the lobsters all desire and want to get out, and they all have the ability to get out, but none of them ever get out- why?'

'Still no takers' I said? (and then I made an impressively genuine sounding buzzer noise)

Oh well time's up.

I explained it 'was because every time one of the lobsters tried to get out, just as it reached the top of the bucket, the rest of the lobsters pull it back in'.
'If they weren't so busy pulling each other back into the bucket, then they could all escape.

I told them that I had seen this 'lobster-syndrome', many times when working with addictions.

A patient from an inner city flat (let's call him 'Shuggy'), who has a heroin addiction, would now be sent off for 6 weeks of residential therapy to a beautiful countryside manor. Before, he knows it then 'Shuggy', will be doing tai-chi every morning, having stunning lunchtime country walks in the garden, Eating 3 course a la carte meals in a feng shui dining room, doing yoga after lunch, learning to express his emotions through the medium of art, sculpture, dance and musical theatre therapy. Then each evening 'Shuggy' would retire off to his king-size four-poster bed, listening to the sound of dolphin music, whilst being guided off to sleep with some sexy white middle-class female voice taking him on a transcendental meditation journey.

And let's face it boys, I said 'Shuggy' would easily not take heroin for 6 weeks.
Unfortunately, within 48 hours of returning back to his inner-city flat, the lobsters would be knocking at 'Shuggy's door' and drag him back into their bucket.
And that boys, is 'lobster syndrome'. I said, 'so watch out for other lobsters in your bucket, because they ultimately are dragging down your potential and will stop you from escaping and getting to the next level in your game'. Therefore, if you do not escape, then you cannot make social changes to your game, and these are required if you want to keep moving forward in your game, rather than slip backwards to where you have been.

However, do not fear boys I said, because there 'is also 'river-otter' syndrome, River otters are socially positive, because when they are in the river they look out for the welfare of the other animals around them. When a river otter spots another animal in danger, then they make a strange noise to warn it to get out of dangers way'.

Positive river otters in your team will communicate with each other to produce a positive safe motivating environment, and they will help the other players to develop faster and push them further towards their potential in the game, by creating a safe friendly space for learning and development. You will know the River otters in your team, because they will improve your levels of motivation, confidence, belief, ambition, connectiveness, resilience and ultimately success levels. 'A good coach should be a river otter and should help coach all his players to become river otters also'.

Earlier, I could see that the boys were surprised at my lack of angry response to their fight at the weekend. I now told them that it was because in a strange way, I knew they were all beginning to become river otters for their 4 other classmates and would try and help each out when they were in danger.

I finished this session, by asking them if they had ever noticed, that when you were young and you told your parents , that you had made a new friend at school today, then they would normally ask straight away 'where do they live' or what do their parents do for a living' or 'what grades do they get at school'. This is your parent's version of the 'lobster and river otter syndrome', they are wanting to make sure that 'your new friend', is in a bucket that will be helpful for you and your future game, and that they are happy for you to be associated with and not just another 'Shuggy'.

'Social buckets are just like football teams, good one's, help you develop faster and better as a player and can push you further towards your potential in the game. Whilst, Bad teams on the other hand, can hinder your confidence, bring down your progress, ambition and motivation and can have real serious consequences on the level of game that you end up playing.

So, I said to them. 'Today we are going to look at who is in your lobster buckets and who is an otter in the river with you?

Positive river otter syndrome = River otters are socially positive, because when they are in the river they look out for the welfare of the other animals around them. When a river otter spots another animal in danger, then they make a strange noise to warn it to get out of dangers way. Positive river otters in the your team communicate with each other to produce a positive safe motivating environment, and they help the other players to develop faster and push them further towards their potential in the game, by creating a safe friendly space for learning and development.
They improve levels of motivation, confidence, belief, ambition, connectiveness, resilience and ultimately success levels.

Negative Lobster bucket syndrome = If you place a few lobsters in a bucket with each other, then none of the lobsters ever manage to escape the bucket, why?
Well, although they all have the ability to climb out and they all desire to get out. They never succeed because each time one is about to get out, the other lobsters pull it back in and the order of whose escaping next changes in a never-ending cycle of failure. The lobsters are the peers that you spend most time with, and the buckets are the places where you spend most time. Negative lobsters (people) and buckets (Places) have the ability to take positive motivating energy from you (or pass negative energy into you), they hinder your confidence, and bring down progress, ambition and motivation. They ultimately drag down your potential and stop you from escaping and getting to the next level in your game.
These negative lobsters actions lead to a decrease in our confidence, happiness, motivation, ambition, belief and success levels

2=Why is your players ability to choose which team of players he associates with and where he spends time playing his game, so important in helping them to keep performing better in the game?

So, In our inner circle of wisdom, I asked them all the question, 'Why do you think as a coach, that it is so important for you to help your player choose the right team to play in and the right places to train their skills in'?

Paulo said= 'So that they can enjoy playing the game'.
Ishmal= 'So that they increase their confidence levels when playing'?
Lennon= 'So that they can learn skills from other different players, which will make them a better overall player'.
Aldous= 'So that they get to challenge their skills against others at a higher level'.
Rocky= 'So that they get the experience of playing in different environments and in different positions with different types of support'. This will give them an idea in which team, role and venue that they play their best game.

Once again, funnily enough, they had collectively nailed the answer.

Yes, I said this 'concept of trying to determine, who helps you play your best game and where, can enable you to experience other players with diverse skills and strengths. This should make you realise that certain people can give you more enjoyment, energy, and support you better when you play the game alongside them. Different venues and teams give you the chance to try different positions and roles in the game, which help you to determine where your skills fit best and in which team you enjoy playing the most and where you seem to be most happy and successful in. This gives you more of a sense of purpose and value within the team and in the game.

I then told them about this female golfer that I had worked with, who whenever she played team-golf, always performed really well and was usually in the winning team. However, she had very limited solo success.

It was quite clear that the isolation of playing alone in tournaments was not very enjoyable or motivating for her and so she lost interest and focus quickly, which then lowered her resilience levels. However, when she played as part of a team, she seemed more inspired and connected and motivated. Which meant her focus and determination levels were a lot higher. It was obvious that she needed to be part of a team to bring out her best skills.

3=Where does our ability to know the difference between a lobster bucket from a river otter come from?

So, I said to the special 5, 'Where do you think our ability to know the difference between a lobster bucket and a river-otter come from?

Or in simpler terms, 'how do we work out what people, players, teams, coaches and training places are helpful to us and which are not?'

Paulo said= (wait for it), 'You get it from your coaches advice'.

Ishmal= 'You get it from knowing how much you enjoy and feel comfortable about playing with different team-mates in different teams'.

Lennon= 'You get it from your parents telling you what teams that you should play in' (I think he may just have stole Aldous's answer).

Aldous= (looking annoyingly at Lennon), 'You get it from counting which teams and coaches are winning the most medals and trophies and then go and join them'.

Rocky said 'Professor, you get it from evaluating your performances and noticing in what positions and teams and pitches that you play your best and get the best results. This will help you to figure out, which environments that you are developing your confidence and ability with at the greatest rate (excellent answer, once again Rocky)

Well done, I said once again all your answers fit perfectly with the question.

'Our ability to know the difference between a lobster bucket and a river-otter, can come from our coaches and our parent's advice about which other support players and teams and positions that they think suit us best. You can also get it from how comfortable you feel playing alongside different players in different teams. It can also come from the results that you visibly see or get with each team you play in. But most importantly, you can get it from the players, coaches and teams where your confidence and ability at playing the game are growing at the fastest rate.

4=How do we measure if our player has the correct level of positive social change (in the correct lobster-bucket) before each game?

So as a coach I said, 'the important thing to remember boys, is that your players (and teams) ability to be a positive stream of river-otters, will enable them to play better for each other as a collective team with a team-goal'. As opposed to dragging each other down in a negative way or just playing for themselves (they all looked at each other and sniggered, obviously, because my last statement sounded like 'playing with yourselves'). They will try harder for the team (another chorus of sneers, which I ignored), and will be more ambitious and motivated for a result. Finally, they will see the benefits of helping each other out with discipline and resilience during changes in the game. They will enjoy the winning as a team more than just winning for themselves also.

So, my next question to all of them was '**As a coach, how will you know if your player has the correct level of positive social connection in the team?'.**
Here were there answers:

Paulo said= 'You ask them what they like best about being in the team?'.
Ishmal= 'You ask them why they think this team helps them play better in the game'?
Lennon= 'You get it from asking them how they are going to help the team win today'?
Aldous = 'You get it from asking them to predict how many goals they think they will score with this team' (he was always about the scoring of goals only).
Rocky= 'Professor, you get it from asking them about how happy they are playing in this team and how valued they feel by the team. As well as, how committed they still feel about helping the team achieve it's purpose of scoring goals and gaining as many victories as possible'.

Great answers I said, 'these are all excellent ways to measure if your player is feeling the correct amount of positive, social connection in order to play well within the team and for the team'.

'You get it from asking them before a new game, what they like best about being part of the team, and why the team is helpful to them. You get it from asking about what they are going to do to help their team win and how much success they feel that the team will help them achieve. Finally, you get it from asking them, how happy and valued they feel playing in the team and how committed they still are, to helping the team achieve its goal or purpose.

I then told them the story of the Premiership footballer that I worked with, and how he would play excellent for his club-team, but when he was playing with his national team he often played poorly and had less influence in the game. This frustrated him, as he would then get a lot of negative feedback from the fans and the national press. This was because they would compare his national team performances to his domestic team performances and think he was not trying as well with the national team. When we worked together it was obvious that the support structure and coaching staff and personalities of his premiership team fitted really well with his personality and style of play, as it gave him the freedom to play to his strengths. However, the national coach played him in a different supporting role in the team and the characters in the national team dressing room were more tense and the atmosphere at the national stadium very different and these were less conducive to him playing to his skills.

We managed to get the national coach to change his role on the pitch, and we did some work in the dressing room to connect the players better and change the atmosphere. Both of these helped completely change his performances and the performances of other players in the squad and within 12 months it had helped the results of the national team.

5= What techniques can we use, to help to improve our players ability to recognize if they are in a lobster-bucket and if so, then get out and move into a stream of river otters?.

Technique 10: The Board-room of your mind.

So I taught them a really simple, yet powerful technique for helping, when you feel your trapped in a bucket in your game and you cannot get out, or you feel that you have no team support (social isolation) or you need a better team of people around you to help you move forward in your game.

I had called this technique **'The Board-room of your mind'**. 'This is where you would close your eyes, and use your mindfulness mask breathing, and now imagine that you are 'managing director of your own club' (which you are), and you are in the board-room of your club.

Next, you need to get your directors into a meeting and ask them 'which players and coaches, that you would need to bring in to coach or play in your team, in order to take your game to the next level'(river-otters). Alternatively in the words of Alan Sugar, you may need to ask ' which players and coaches you may 'need to fire', from the team and your club (Lobsters), as they are being unhelpful to its continued improvement.

The other directors will be relevant role-models to the situation, and can be famous people you admire, people you know in life, imaginary characters from books and films, but they need to be people who you think would provide you with helpful information and act like river-otters for you. You then ask them the question which other players or coaches in real-life, that they would think that you need to connect and spend more time with, in order to move your game and your club forward to the next desired destination.

Then you commit that week to seek out connections or spend time with those coaches or other players

In reality, I said boys 'this could be a variety of connections that people would need to make socially to help them. For example, it could be; support groups, professional mind-coaches, physical trainers, weight loss specialist, counsellors, work colleagues, family members, old friends, medical professions, addiction workers, the Samaritans or church-members.

So now I said to the boys,' I all want you to practising this technique and working out which one person this week, you need to connect and spend more time with, as they could help move your game forward. To aid with this exercise I played them the song, 'Holding out for a hero', by Bonnie Tyler.

'If you all put your mindfulness masks on and close your eyes, now imagine that you are the managing director of your own club (which you are).
Now place yourself in the boardroom and start to choose any 4 Directors that you think will help provide you with good information on which coaching staff or player, that you should invite to spend more time at your club this week as it will help your game move forward'.

I gave them all 5 minutes for this exercise. Out of personal courtesy, then I never asked them to mention who it was that they had committed to connect with or spend more time with this week. I asked them to repeat this exercise each night before they went to bed. They may just find it useful to their future.

Afterwards, I wanted them to write down the people they spend most time with at the moment and then rate whether each of them was a lobster or a river-otter.
Then I asked them to make a list of the people who would be most helpful for them to spend time with at present. They were then to think about how much time they were actually spending with them and how much the extra time they should spend. Then I said, 'maybe you can take some of your time away from the lobsters and give it to these river-otters instead.

I ended this session by saying to the boys in the circle. 'We all have times when we are faced with helping our team-mates out, even if it will cause us pain or discomfort or get us into trouble (I looked around at their cut, bruised and blackened features). Because playing in a team, is so much more rewarding than playing yourself (once again the chuckles echoed around the room).

But you always need to keep asking yourself, if you are playing in good helpful teams with good other players, who also share your common purpose of moving forward in their game. You need to constantly ensure that you are in teams that are moving you forward to your desired destination in the game and still making you enjoy and feel confident playing in their team game. It is also important that you understand the enjoyment that comes from being a helpful team-mate, who helps others to reach new levels in their game.

Yes boys, always check that you are still swimming in a river of otters or you may just find yourself caught and trapped in a bucket of lobsters.

I asked the boys to look up at the map on the wall again and I summarized by saying

This week we discussed why it is important to have good people in your car or on your bus when you are making a journey, as makes the journey easier and more enjoyable.

I then asked the boys again this week if 'anyone had found the £10,000 treasure box', which the head coach Frank had hidden someone in the camp and the clue to its whereabouts was;
'The sooner that you can see the process, then the next part of the journey will unveil itself and the treasure will be found'.

They all groaned as ever "NO".

Then I proceeded to award them their fantasy class scores for this session and I wrote these up on the wall next to their fantasy football scores then

The boys as always moaned about their class scores and pointed out that their class results, did not mirror their football results, but as I always said to them
'Guys, there is a still a lot of time left for you to play in the game and who says that I am talking about football!.

And as they all went noisily out of the room, I reminded them
'Remember boys, 'You never lose in this game, you only win or you learn'.
They were too busy talking to care.

Moving forward in our life Journey?

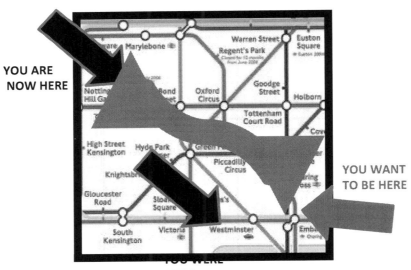

YOU ARE
NOW HERE

YOU WANT
TO BE HERE

YOU WERE
HERE

Week 10 Fantasy football results

Name	Value	Points this week in game	Total points from all games	Current Rating out of the 22 players
Aldous	30 mill	8	91	1st
Rocky	10 mill	8	81	4th
Paulo	15 mill	7	76	7th
Lennon	5 mill	7	64	10th
Ishmal	1 mill	6	60	12th

Week 10 Fantasy class results

Name	Value	Points this week in class	Total points from all classes	Current Rating out of the 5 in class
Rocky	10 mill	9	93	1st
Paulo	15 mill	7	73	2nd
Ishmal	1 mill	7	66	3rd
Lennon	5 mill	4	40	4th
Aldous	30 mill	3	30	5th

Chapter 17= Social resilience versus social submission-

PILARS LAW 11=*The most successful of any species are those who can adapt quickest and best to changes in their environment.*

'insanity is doing the same thing Again but expecting a different result-**Albert einstein**

When I entered the classroom this Monday morning, there was no one there? Which was odd as the boys were normally in class before me. I waited for 10 minutes before going to see where they were. I found them in Franks office.
Lennon had smashed up a toilet hand-dryer, punched a hole in his bedroom wall and door and kicked a television over (putting an end to its working life). I could tell that Frank was not impressed and he looked at me with eyes that said, 'I thought you were meant to be helping these boys to manage their emotions better'.
I told Frank that I would have a word with Lennon, but that I felt it was better for all the boys to be in class just now, rather than serve them some kind of a detention. Frank agreed but shot a piercing glare at Lennon and told him 'that his parents would be paying for the damage'.
Lennon, uncharacteristically just shrugged his shoulders and said 'whatever, I don't care either way'.
I could see that Frank was ready to fly across his desk and do a bit of damage of his own (and he was a large powerful man), so I quickly stepped in and marched Lennon and the other boys to my classroom.
As we sat in our circle of wisdom, I asked Lennon 'what was all that about', he said 'he didn't want to talk about it' and then proceeded to start crying in front of the others. As he cried, he started to mumble incoherently, but I could roughly tell what he was saying 'His mum had phoned him this morning saying

that she had left his father, and they were getting a divorce'. She had also mentioned that 'she had met someone else in Wales and they would be moving there when he got back from summer camp in 2 weeks time'.

He divulged to the group that his dad was a lousy drunk and would occasionally beat on his mum, but that sober he was a decent guy and he never thought his mum would leave him.

Lennon had obviously decided to re-decorate his bedroom door, wall, TV and bathroom after that phone-call this morning.

I thought it would be useful to go around the group in a clockwise fashion and ask the boys 'what they thought about this situation and what would they do If they were in Lennon's position'?

Paulo= said 'he would phone his dad to check and see if he is okay and then refuse to move to wales with his mum'.

Ishmal= said that 'he would maybe check with his mum, to see if she had just reacted because she was fed up taking the abuse from his dad, but that she would maybe come back once she had calmed down and his dad agreed to seek help for his drinking and violence'.

Aldous= said 'he would go to wales and knock out this new fancy man' ('unhelpful Aldous', I said).

Rocky= said that 'he would try and forget about it until after camp, as there is nothing he could do to change it at the moment. But when he got home from camp, then he would sit down with both his parents and discuss if things were repairable or not. If not, then he could just plan the next stage of his life, because he may get signed at the end of summer-camp anyway, and have to move away on his own to a new football club in a new city'.

I mentioned that I thought all their contributions were useful (apart from Aldous's).
We then quickly discussed their game at the weekend. It had been a 2-2 draw, but Aldous was still sitting at the top of the fantasy football league. Rocky was now in 3rd position, Paulo 7th, Lennon 9th and Ishmal 13th out of the 22 players at camp. Their class results were Rocky, then Paulo, then Ishmal, Lennon and Aldous.
But remember I said in my humorous tone **' don't worry boys, as there is still a lot of time left to play in the game yet, and who said that I am talking about football**. This was the first time that they actually laughed with me to this line (I had finally worn them down).

This made me remember 'Tuckmans' theory of group stages and I realized that I had just witnessed a poignant moment in this groups development. According to Tuckman, there had been loads of norming and storming in the class, but this was the first time that the boys had performed the laugh with me. However, with only 1 week to go we would soon be adjourning and then mourning.
I finished by saying, well in today's 11th session of the certificate course **'so you think you could be a coach'**, then we will be talking about: The power of 'social resilience and repetition' and its opposing skill 'social submission and rejection'.
I could see by their morose faces, that they couldn't wait to get cracking on this subject.

Week 11 Fantasy football results

Name	Value	Points this week in game	Total points from all games	Current Rating out of the 22 players
Aldous	30 mill	7	98	1st
Rocky	10 mill	9	90	3rd
Paulo	15 mill	7	83	7th
Lennon	5 mill	7	71	9th
Ishmal	1 mill	6	66	13th

Week 11 Fantasy class results

Name	Value	Points this week in class	Total points from all classes	Current Rating out of the 5 in class
Rocky	10 mill	9	102	1st
Paulo	15 mill	8	81	2nd
Ishmal	1 mill	7	73	3rd
Lennon	5 mill	4	44	4th
Aldous	30 mill	3	33	5th

1= Definition of social resilience versus social submission.

I pointed up to the map on the wall and summarized what we had covered so far:

-**Awareness** is knowing where you currently are on the map and how far away that is from where you would like to be.

-**Ambition** is wanting to move forward in the future, to another desired destination.

-**Goals** are the travel route-plan of those specific places that you need to reach first, which lie between where you are and where your desired destination is.

-**Attitude** is thinking it is important enough now, to leave your current location and commit spending your focus, energy, skill and time moving on to reach your next goal .

-**Focus** is being able to keep your mind concentrated on staying on the correct route to your next goal.

-**Motivators** are the fuel which will keep you moving forward on your route to the next goal.

-**Beliefs** give you the **confidence** that your journey will reach the desired destination

-**Physical Change commitment** starts the Physical journey to the next goal'

-**Physical Resilience** helps you to keep getting out in the rain to fix a flat tyre, whenever you get one, and then get back in your car to carry on with the physical journey to your desired destination.

-**Physical Results** are like watching the video highlights of all the beautiful scenery and amazing landmarks that you have already seen on the journey now, and they help us to keep physically want to keep going on further, to see what amazing things we may find at the next goal destination

Social change buckets= These are the people that you have with you in the car on your bus as you travel towards your desired destinations.

And today we will discuss **'Social resilience'**. Last week we spoke about when you want to make a social change, then you need to start to make a change to your social bucket, or who you are spending time with. This week then the social resilience is the ability to keep trying and repeating a change in social situations with others and not get dragged back into the lobster bucket. I said boys ' on the improvement journey map this is the equivalent of having to share public transport or share a hostel and talk with new people, and although you don't want to, you need to repeat doing it in order to keep moving forwards, until you reach your desired destination.

Social Submission = This is your ability to keep socially quiet or secret about wanting to improve your game, because you believe that you may get visible social results at this time. These actions lead to an decrease in our social confidence, social-support, belief, ambition, connectiveness, social knowledge and skills, resilience and ultimately success levels, but an increase in our social isolation.

Social resilence Repetition = Your ability to keep socially repeating the improvement process despite a lack of visible social results at this time. This improves levels of social confidence, belief, ambition, social-support, connectiveness, social knowledge and skills, resilience and ultimately success levels.

I said to the boys, 'Something tells me, that you have all heard the phrase 'you need to speak up for yourself, and start thinking for yourself, as you are too easily led'?
But why do you think parents and coaches say that to you?
All 5 boys looked at me like I had suddenly morphed into their parents and they all shrugged their shoulders in unison and groaned, 'we have no idea'.
After the deadly silence, (it was obvious that they literally had no idea). Then I proceeded to tell the boys, that research has

shown that 'in most cases when people wish to change or improve their game, then they cannot keep it a social secret'. Those who do not tell others that they are wanting to change or trying to improve their game usually do not succeed. Those that do tell their team-mates and lobster bucket associates, that they are trying to change or improve their game have 4 times the likelihood of success (80% successful versus only 20% success in people who tried to improve their game alone and in silence).

So why is this? I looked up to see if any one of them were remotely interested in trying to give me an answer (that would be a negative then).

Well, I said (trying to look like their silence was a planned part of this session), ' it is because in order to build your social resilience to making changes or improvements in your game, then you need to keep socially repeating your improvement every day for around 8 weeks before they become social habits (your next final session). Therefore, if you do not show anyone else in your lobster buckets, that you are changing and wanting out of the bucket, then they will naturally try to drag you back in, as they are not aware that you want help to get out.

I told them that the biggest indicator in any addiction that someone who has quit, and will go back to their old behaviours, is not anything about the individual themselves, but rather, it is the amount of lobsters who they are still spending time with, who have the addiction, but who they have not yet told, that they have quit or are trying to quit. The reason they try and keep it a secret and do not tell others that they have changed, is that they are worried they will fail again and then have to admit it to everyone that they never managed it. Or they do not want to tell, as they are worried that the other lobsters in the bucket, might judge them for wanting to be different. However social resilience is the ability to proudly tell others that you are wanting to move forward on your journey, and even if you end up failing and going back to an old destination, then you pick yourself up and tell them you will try to move forward again. This will develop your social resilience, which is the ability to keep repeating to others without worry or shame that you are trying to move forward on your journey and improve your game, no matter how many hurdles get in your way.

That is why your coaches and parents will often tell you that you 'need to speak up and think for yourself'. As they do not want other lobsters dragging you back into unhelpful buckets or causing your abilities in the game to get dragged down, because they had no idea that you were wanting to change, as you did not speak up and tell them.

2=Why is your players ability to socially repeat the improvement process, so important in helping them to keep performing better in the game?

So, In our inner circle of wisdom, I asked them all the question, 'Why do you think as a coach, that it is important for you to help your players, to keep socially repeating the improvement process, in order for them to perform better in the game'?

Paulo said= 'So that they can understand that repetition is the best way of improving their game'.

Ishmal= 'So that they increase their social confidence levels as they will be practicing in front of others when playing'?

Lennon= 'So that they can learn skills from watching other different players play, as they practice'.

Aldous= 'So that they increase the social awareness of their skills to other scouts and managers, and get picked for a better team'.

Rocky= 'So that they get experiences of success and failures in front of others, but that this keeps them determined and increases their levels of resilience and ambition and motivation to keep improving their game, regardless of what others think'. (another wonderful answer from Rocky)

Once again collectively they had pretty much nailed the answer.

Yes, I said this 'concept of trying to nurture your player to enjoy socially repeating the process of improving their game is very helpful in enhancing their ability to keep repeating change, to become more socially confident at trying change in front of others, as well as learning abilities from watching others socially practice change. It helps your player to become visible to other players, coaches and teams, as someone who is ambitious and wants to improve their game, therefore they will then tend to attract others who are motivated to improve their game also (river-otters). Finally, social experiences of repeating change improvement to your own game is a great way for your player to learn social resilience and to learn that performing for their own self-development and happiness, is more important than worrying what others think of your social performance in the game.

I then told them about a snooker payer that I had once worked with.

He had contacted me because when he was in the snooker hall on his 'training table', playing alone he could routinely score 147 maximum breaks, but when it came to televised competitions, then he could rarely get breaks of more than 50 going.

I asked him why he thought this happened?

He told me that the extra pressure of the crowd and the lights and the camera's and the other players as competition got him over-stressed and over-excited and then his focus would

change. This change in his focus resulted in him slightly mis-hitting the first ball, and although it would go into the pocket, he would find he was now further away and more out of position away from his next ball than he would have liked. This would add another bit of stress onto him and so his focus would lower again, which meant his the next shot would get less accurate again and although the ball would go in, he was now even further away from the position he wanted to be in for potting his next ball. Anyway, this series of getting stressed and losing focus and systematically getting further out of position with each new ball, would eventually lead to him not being in position at all and his run would be finished on the table.

It was clear to me that that he was allowing the change in social environment to change his mindset (he was doing exactly the same thing in both scenarios i.e. hitting balls on a snooker table into snooker pockets). But his mind was focused on socially caring about the lights, cameras, audience and other players in competition, and got him worried about social failure in these conditions, whereas in his local snooker hall, he was not worried about social failure and so he felt no pressure and would routinely make breaks of 147 on the table. In essence, he was allowing the situation to manage him and his emotional state and focus level, rather than allow himself to see both situations as the same and thus play the same. We taught him to blank out the pressure of the social environment by getting him to practice in the open public, with people watching him and making noises and laughing. He got so used to playing in this social environment that it increased his social resilience to pressures. Needless to say, he went on that year and won the world championships.

3=Where does our ability to be able to keep socially repeating the improvement process come from?

So, I said to the special 5, 'Where do you think our desire to keep socially repeating the improvement process come from? or 'how do we nurture more of this 'social repetition of the improvement process in our player'?

Paulo said= 'They get it from their coaches training'.

Ishmal= 'They get it from their team-mates wanting to keep getting better'.

Lennon= 'They get it from enjoying practicing in front of other people'.

Aldous= 'They get it from their parents telling them that they need to keep showing that they are better than everyone else' (Parent issues again).

Rocky = 'Professor, they get it from enjoying constructive feedback and praise from others about their performance, as well as evaluating their performances and the performances of others, to see what areas they could put more time and effort into improving to enhance their overall game.

I said once again as a collective team you have made a great effort guys.

The ability of your player to desire to keep socially repeating the improvement process can come from their coaches, parents and team-mates. It can also be nurtured by enjoying practicing in front of others and gaining constructive feedback and deserved praise for their performances. Whilst also being developed from evaluating themself and other people's performances, to determine what areas that they could still focus more time and energy into improving to give them an overall better game.

4=How do we measure if our player has the social resilience for improvement before each game?

So as a coach, I said 'the important thing to remember is that your players (and teams) ability to socially repeat being resilient in the improvement process before each game, is important because it will help them to play better with each other as a collective team. They will try harder for the team, be more ambitious and motivated for a result, help each other with discipline and resilience and be able to keep going no matter what hurdles appear in the game.

So, my next question to all of them became '**As a coach, how do you measure if your player has enough social resilience for improvement before each game?**

Here were there answers:

Paulo said= 'You watch the effort they have put into their training sessions this week'.

Ishmal= 'You watch their attitude in the dressing room as they socially interact with their team-mates and tell them about the improvements that they have been working on

Lennon= 'You get it from asking them, what part of their game that they have been working on this week and why'? (Lennon, had actually been listening to me this week).

Aldous = 'You get it from asking them to predict how well they will play today'.

Rocky= 'Professor, you get it from asking about what they hope to achieve from the game today, and how will they know that their training this week has helped them to play against this particular opponent'.

Excellent I said, 'as these are all ways to measure your players level of social resilience for improvement before each game'. You get it from watching the effort that they put into training (did they turn up early, or stay later to practice even more), I reminded them, what the coach told me about the world's best football player. You can also get their social resilience levels by getting them to tell their teammates before the game, what they have been working on to improve their game.

You can get it from asking them what improvements they have been personally working on and why? You get it from asking them 'how well they think they will play today based on their improvement work. Finally you can get it from asking what they hope to achieve against this opponent and how will they know that they have achieved it.

5= What techniques can we use, to help to improve our players ability for social resilience to the improvement process?

Technique 11: Buzzwire Social Resilience Technique.

So, I taught the boys a simple fun technique for improving your social resilience and focus on continuing to improve your performance even in the face of adversity and social pressure to give up.

I brought into the classroom the classic children's game Buzzwire.

In this game there is a complex convoluted metal wire which spans across two columns. The wire has electricity running through it and the aim of the game is for the player to weave a small handle from one column to the other travelling through the middle of complex wire shape without touching the wire or the electricity connection causes a buzzer to go off.

I said to the boys 'This is a relatively easy exercise, if you are on your own with no noise or distraction or anyone watching you or laughing at you for failing'.

But guess what boys I said, 'Today you will all be increasing your ability for social resilience to continued improvement, by playing this game. However, you will be getting shouted at, booed, laughed at and distracted by your social peers in this class'. If you hit the wire then you will need to go back to the start and try again, you will keep repeating going back, until you have managed to do it from one end to the other without touching the wire. This will prove that you have mastered the art of complete focus and the social resilience of being able to keep repeating an exercise until you succeed, even in the face of social pressure and humiliation and distraction.

I then played the song 'under pressure', by David Bowie and Queen, And So the fun and games began....
It took about an hour before all 5 of them had managed it, But, they did it in good spirits and they all seemed to enjoy it. I also sensed that they gained from the exercise, as they all seemed to look less intimidated by social failure now, and more open to knowing that often you need to repeat things in life before you improve at them or succeed at them.

I finished the session, by saying to the boys, 'that you can never fully change or improve or move forward in your journey unless you socially repeat the change or improvement and people see that you have socially moved forward out of your lobster bucket.

I then pleaded with them to never underestimate the power of social repetition in their own lives, even if people mock you or laugh at you or do not believe you can do something, or your social environment are not helpful to you changing. This is when you need to keep socially repeating it just like you did in here, with your buzzwire game and remember you all got there in the end, even though the other people around you and the social environment were trying to be unhelpful and stop you.
I then turned to Lennon and said' Lennon, I am sorry to hear about your mum and dad and I am unsure what will happen next to them, but you are on our own journey and I want you to focus on your own map and the journey that you want to make from now on, because that is the only one that you can control. If your parents are river-otters then they will still be with you every step of the way on your journey.

I asked the boys to look up at the map on the wall again and I summarized by saying

'This week we discussed why it is important to keep socially repeating improvement so that others know where you wish to go next, and the important people will help you on the journey. Social resilience is the equivalent of having to keep asking to hitch a ride with helpful strangers because your car has currently broken down and been towed to the next destination. However, you need to overcome the embarrassment or humiliation of having to keep hitching a ride, until you can get to the next destination and be reunited with your car.

I then asked the boys again this week if 'anyone had found the £10,000 treasure box', which the head coach Frank had hidden someone in the camp and The clue to its whereabouts was;
'The sooner that you can see the process, then the next part of the journey will unveil itself and the treasure will be found'.

They all groaned as ever "NO".

Then I proceeded to award them their fantasy class scores for this session and I wrote these up on the wall next to their fantasy football scores then
The boys as always moaned about their class scores and pointed out that their class results, did not mirror their football results, but as I always said to them
'Guys, there is a still a lot of time left for you to play in the game and who says that I am talking about football!.

And as they all went buzzing out of the room, I reminded them
'Remember boys, 'You never lose in this game, you only win or you learn'.
They were too happy to bother.

Week 11 Fantasy football results

Name	Value	Points this week in game	Total points from all games	Current Rating out of the 22 players
Aldous	30 mill	7	98	1st
Rocky	10 mill	9	90	3rd
Paulo	15 mill	7	83	7th
Lennon	5 mill	7	71	9th
Ishmal	1 mill	6	66	13th

Week 11 Fantasy class results

Name	Value	Points this week in class	Total points from all classes	Current Rating out of the 5 in class
Rocky	10 mill	9	102	1st
Paulo	15 mill	8	81	2nd
Ishmal	1 mill	7	73	3rd
Lennon	5 mill	4	44	4th
Aldous	30 mill	3	33	5th

Chapter 18= social success versus regretful relapse

PILARS LAW 12= *The law of entropy, is that if you put excessive stress on a system, then it will either cause the system to collapse under the pressure and cease to exist or the structure will transform and convert itself into another form which can now withstand the pressure.*

"When we are no longer able to change a situation, then we are challenged to change ourselves."
— *Viktor E. Frankl*

This was my final session of the 12 week summer-camp. The boys would just play their final game in front of the Premiership club scouts and then their 12 weeks of 'hell' would be over.

I had mixed feelings about my 12 weeks, I had thoroughly enjoyed working with the 5 boys, but I often felt like I was an outsider at camp and my classes were the least important of all the coaches (I perceived them to be the total opposite of course). But it had been a glorious summer of weather and I had enjoyed my time back in Oxford.

When I entered the class, the boys were all sitting nervously and looking dumbfounded. I asked them 'what was wrong' and Aldous answered 'nothing'.

I could see a few of them looking uncomfortable and nudging Aldous to tell me.

So, I said 'Aldous, is there anything you want to tell me?". Once again he repeated 'No' and so I was about to leave it and move on, when Lennon said' Aldous he may be able to give you some advice'. Aldous gave him a horrifying look back, and then a after a few seconds he spoke up and said' Professor (it was the first time that he had ever called me this), 'My girlfriend phoned me this morning and told me that she is pregnant'. There was a deadly silence in the room at these words (I got the feeling that a few of the others were empathizing about how this phone call would have felt for them). I said ' okay, does she know for definite?

Aldous replied ' Yes it looks definite'.

Then I asked ' How do you feel about her, can you see her in your long term future?'

Aldous replied' yes she is nice enough, but I don't know' (I took this as a no).

Well first of all, my advice would be to concentrate on your final game here at summer camp and forget about it until your finished here. There is nothing you can do about that situation at the moment, but there is a lot you can do about getting picked up by a premiership team and helping the future of you, the girl and the baby. I told Aldous' I know that is easier said than done, but you need to keep focused on what important things you can control at the moment for moving forward in your game'. Finally, I asked him to look at the map and I said 'Aldous, having a child will definitely alter your journey on this map now'.

I then deliberately changed the subject and said 'has anyone found the £10,000 treasure box', which the head coach Frank had hidden someone in the camp and The clue to its whereabouts was;

'The sooner that you can see the process, then the next part of the journey will unveil itself and the treasure will be found'. They all groaned as ever "NO".

Then I proceeded to award them their fantasy class scores for this session and I wrote these up on the wall next to their fantasy football scores then

The boys as always moaned about their class scores and pointed out that their class results, did not mirror their football results, but as I always said to them

'Guys, there is a still a lot of time left for you to play in the game and who says that I am talking about football!.

And I reminded them 'Remember boys, 'You never lose in this game, you only win or you learn'.

So I carried on, 'in this final 12th session we will be talking about the final stage of change, which is sustaining 'social success'.
I said 'if you look up to the map on the wall', then this is the equivalent on the map of finally getting to your desired destination. As opposed to 'regretful relapse', which is when you end up back at a previous location and regret leaving your desired destination.

Moving forward in our life Journey?

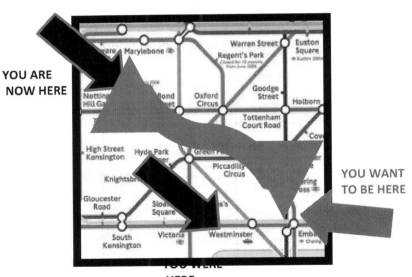

Week 12 Fantasy football results

Name	Value	Points this week in game	Total points from all games	Current Rating out of the 22 players
Aldous	30 mill	7	105	1st
Rocky	10 mill	9	99	4th
Paulo	15 mill	7	90	7th
Lennon	5 mill	6	77	11th
Ishmal	1 mill	8	74	14th

Week 12 Fantasy class results

Name	Value	Points this week in class	Total points from all classes	Current Rating out of the 5 in class
Rocky	10 mill	10	112	1st
Paulo	15 mill	9	90	2nd
Ishmal	1 mill	7	80	3rd
Lennon	5 mill	4	48	4th
Aldous	30 mill	3	36	5th

1= Definition of social success versus regretful relapse

I said to the boys, Something tells me, that you have all heard the phrases 'why is it when I play my best game, there is never anyone there to see it, or when I score a great goal everyone seems to be looking in the other direction and they miss it', or when the scouts come to watch me then I always play my worst game '.

They all nodded in agreement.
This often is a problem when people have improved their game. We need others to socially recognize our success, in order for us to want to keep them as new habits. Social attractiveness is the concept of feeling that you have socially improved yourself in the eyes of others. We need people to recognise that we are now more socially attractive because of our new social success in order for us to want to keep these as new social habits. A social success is when an improvement has been completed and is engrained as an intrinsic part of you and your daily life now. If We do not feel that the success has made us more socially attractive, then we tend to give up on it and relapse back to our old behavior and these regretful relapses can be source of frustration to many players.
So the last part of the journey boys 'is enjoying the new social successful change and having people recognise it as a positive addition to your life'.
I tried to reinforce this theory by telling them that research has shown that when people get socially complimented by others on their self-improvements or other people find them more socially attractive due to new improvements, then it makes it 4 times more likely that they will maintain the new social success change and embed it into their everyday lives now.
(80% more likely to maintain a habit when others have complimented you on it versus only 20% success in maintaining

a habit, when non-on else has commented on it being a positive social addition to you).

So for the purposes of your certificate course ' **So you think you could be a coach?"**
Then the definitions we will use in this class is:

Social success is defined as your ability to maintain a new social change due to experiencing social results and benefits and increasing your social attractiveness.

Regretful relapse is defined as your ability to relapse back to an old behaviour, due to not experiencing social results and benefits and feelings that your social attractiveness was increased.

2=Why is your players ability to sustain new improved social habits, so important in helping them to keep performing better in the game?

So, In our inner circle of wisdom, I asked them all the question, 'Why do you think as a coach, that it is important for you to help ensure that your players, know how far they have developed and improved their game, in order for them to keep performing better in the game'?
Paulo said= 'So that they can feel proud of themselves and their achievements'.
Ishmal= 'So that they realise that all the effort they have put in has been worth it and so they will want to keep trying to add even more new social improvements into their game in the future'.
Lennon= 'So that they can inspire other people who have seen their improvements and go on and become role-models for other younger players in the team'.
Aldous= 'So that they can enjoy hearing people say how good they are at playing the game'.

Rocky= 'So that every time they get a compliment about their abilities in playing the game, they can reflect on the journey of change improvement that they have been on, and enjoy recalling the highs and lows and how they kept training their motivation and resilience and ambition levels to keep going. This will keep their momentum going to inspire a life-time of enjoying developing their game to its full potential.
'Good effort Rocky' I said

'Yes, it is important for a coach to ensure that players know how far they have travelled in their development in the game. It helps them to feel proud of the work they have put in, and this pride can help to build new ambitions in producing more improvement. It helps them to want to become role-models for inspiring improvement in other players. It gives them an energy-boost when others appreciate and admire their skills in the game. It helps them reflect on the journey of change that they have been on and they can enjoy recalling the attributes that they have trained in themselves including ambition, confidence, belief, motivation and resilience. This self-reflection on their journey and increases their ambition to want to produce further developments in their game and help others develop their game also.

I told the boys 'this is why in the addictions world, people once they have not taken a drug for 12 months are often encouraged to go on and help or buddy others to quit. It is because in this process they get to realise the power of their own achievements and how well they have done and this gives them a responsibility for helping and sharing their success with others, whilst not letting people down by going backwards themselves.
Part of the reason we ask them to help others is to really help themselves.

I then told them about a story about a guy who stabbed someone and who went to prison, but unlike the rest of the guys he met in Jail, who had also been imprisoned for serious

assault and who just spent their time still trying to get drunk and high and fight. This guy started reading self-help and doing self-development programs, then he studied for a degree whilst in prison and when all the inmates were finally released, he was the only one of them who managed to get a job and create a good life for himself. Within 1 year the other guys were either dead or back in prison or addicted to drugs.

The point of the story I told the boys was 'that it wasn't important where they all had been, the important thing is knowing where you would like to be next and then your ability to read your future-map to see where you need to travel to first, in order to reach your next desired destination and then enjoy the journey along the way.

Moving forward in our life Journey?

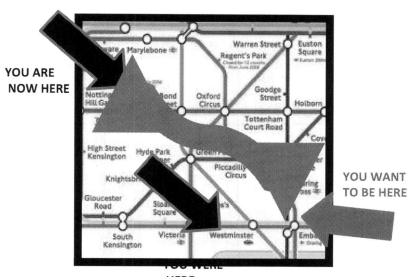

YOU ARE NOW HERE

YOU WANT TO BE HERE

YOU WERE HERE

3=Where does our ability to be able to sustain social success come from?

So, I said to the special 5, 'where do you think our ability to be able to sustain social success changes come from'?

Paulo said= (for the final time) 'We get it from our coaches'.

Ishmal= 'We get it from enjoying the benefits of the new social change that we are willing to do all we can to keep it going'.

Lennon= 'We get it from remembering the consequences of what it would be like going back to having a worse game or being in a worse teams if we don't keep the change going'.

Aldous= 'We get it from enjoying the admiration and adoration of people who wished that they had our skill at playing the game'.

Rocky= 'Professor, we get it from enjoying where are on our journey and being proud of how far we have travelled in developing our abilities in playing the game, so that we can now look forward to the next place where we want to be and this stops us looking or travelling backwards'.

Yes, in summary you are all correct I said, 'The ability of your player to sustain social success changes; comes from our coaches, from the results we have already gained, from the adoration of others, from the fear of having to go back as a worse player In a worse team. Finally, we get it from recalling our journey with pride and enjoying where we are at present as it is nicer than where we have been'.

4=How do we measure if our player has the ability to sustain social success before each game?

So as a coach I said, 'the important thing to remember is that your players (and teams) ability to sustain social success (or winning habits), is important because it will help them to keep playing better and want to keep developing as an improved player with each game. The team will also keep wanting to win. Success breeds success and players will try harder, be more ambitious and motivated to play for a successful team.

So my next question to all of them became '**As a coach, How do you measure if your player has the ability to maintain social success (winning habits) before each game?**
Here were there answers:

Paulo said= 'You watch the effort they have put into their training sessions this week'.
Ishmal= 'You watch to see if they are improving their skill in training'.
Lennon= You get it from seeing how they now help try and improve the younger players in the team
Aldous= 'You get it from seeing their increased ambition now, as they want to become the captain of the team, and become the best player possible'.
Rocky= 'Professor, you get it from asking them what aspect of their game, that they are most proud that they have improved and why has this made them a better player in the game'.

'Excellent' I said you now all think and talk like certified coaches.

.

5= What techniques can we use, to help to improve our players ability to sustain success changes before each game.

Technique 12: The Song Playlist of your Journey.

One final technique I wanted to show them, so that their future self could always be reminded of their past selves Successes in the game so far.

I told them to put on their mindfulness masks and start relax breathing (and do some progressive muscle relaxation). Then I wanted them to commit from now on that whenever they had video footage of a great performance, or a photo of them in a success moment or they had a great memory of success, then they would do this exercise and take that memory into to their own mind using the 'Managing directors boardroom again, (because we all are managing directors of our own club and our own game). I told them in their minds Managing Directors boardroom, to get that video playing on the large TV, or that Photo hanging up in the wall or that trophy or medal on the shelfs. But the important thing now to do, was to link hearing a different song playing when you looked at each and every one of these previous successes. That way whenever you heard the song in the future you would instantly be reminded of your past selves success, or if you wanted to trigger the memory instantly yourself, then all you just needed to do was to play the song on your music device and the success memory would come flooding back.

This I told them 'would become, 'The playlist of their Journey', and would eventually contain past, present and future songs, all linked to the highlights of their journey across the map and within their game. To aid them in this exercise I played the song 'live like you were dying', by Tim McGraw.

When they all finished this exercise and opened their eyes and took off their mindfulness masks. Then I could swear that I saw a change in all of them. At this moment, I genuinely believe, that they had all realized that even at 16 years of age, they had already contributed some success to their game.

One final technique I wanted them to learn in order to help them keep focused more on all the little daily social successes. They were to add these recurrences on daily repeat to their calendars on their phone. Each morning they would write one thing for each of these 4 entries:

-1 past positive memory I will think of today
-1 thing I want to enjoy about today
-1 future GOAL that I have
-1 thing I could do today that would move me forward towards a GOAL of mine

And then Each night they would write one thing for each of these 2 entries:
-1 good deed I did today,
-The highlight of the day,

They looked at me, liked I had asked them to dig a ditch every morning before breakfast.

So I realized, that I needed to convince them more, I said' each of these 6 entries will help you enjoy each day more, appreciate each day more, be more productive each day, and more grateful for each day'. Then I stated, 'that's not a bad result for something which takes less than a minute of your time up each day'.

This exercise boys I said, 'is the equivalent of swallowing a medical miracle pill each day, which makes you feel better, happier more energized and helps you live longer'.

I could see they were even less convinced now.

So, I decided to finish the session on that medical bombshell.

As I looked around at these 5 bright-eyed and engaged, energized faces, I couldn't believe that it was the same 5 gormless idiots who I had first met 12 weeks ago.

I was so proud of each of them, like they were my own children. I told them of my pride in being part of their short journey.

They asked me 'what was next'? And I said 'you are now all free to go' this Mind-fitness and game-mindset bootcamp is now over for summer.

I told them 'that I would now write a report on each of them and this would include my future predictions on how far each of them could go in the game', as this was part of my research project with them.

I told them that they will play different roles in the game as they move through life. That each of these roles requires you to successfully change your mindset and behaviours and your goals, or the game could crush you. At the moment they are young players still getting coached, then they will become senior players who play their own way, then they may become coaches of their own young players, then overseeing manager of a team and hopefully one day sit happily up in the Directors box enjoying watching the new generations of their team and club play on the field, whilst they clap them on and hope to see them win some trophies also, like they did in their day.

I knew they were all itching to leave class, as it was their final match tomorrow, and maybe the most important game in their life so far, as all the premiership club scouts would be there and it was still to be decided on 'who would win the best player at summer-camp from the fantasy league tables'. I asked them who they thought would win 'man of the match tomorrow'. They all shouted back 'Aldous'.

In truth, every one of us would have been very surprised in that moment, if we had known who actually would win 'man of the match'.

There was nothing left, but that uncomfortable 'goodbye' silence, that especially lingers between males who do not know how to be sincere or emotional or do not have the confidence to look sad at leaving someone else.

I was almost jealous that all these fine young peacocks were just starting out on what could be the most exciting stages of their game, and that premiership football and fortune and fame may await them.

I laughed and said to each of them 'give us a manly hug goodbye then' and they all queued up one by one. Aldous sheepishly stayed at the back and to this day, I still swear that I felt that he wanted to say something to me or ask me something, but he hesitated at the last minute and never had the courage to say it.

Moving forward in our life Journey?

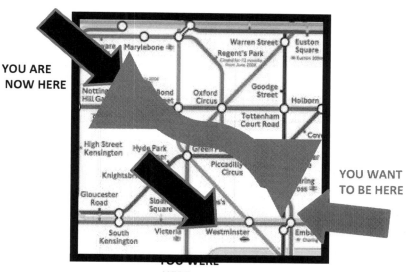

YOU ARE
NOW HERE

YOU WANT
TO BE HERE

YOU WERE
HERE

Chapter 19: The Final Game

'The best way to predict the future is to create it'
-Peter drucker

 The clue where frank had hidden the £1000 cash treasure box had said **" the sooner that you can see the process then the next part of the journey will unveil itself and the treasure will be found.**
On the final day, Rocky cleverly worked out that frank had hidden the cash-box in a hole In The wall behind the large London Underground map hanging in my classroom (in fairness, I had been pointing the 5 boys to it for 12 weeks now).
The big day had finally arrived and it was the last Sunday of summer camp , which meant the deciding football game of summer camp. For some of these boys it may be the most important game of their life as this was the match that the premiership scouts were attending and therefore some of these boys could be premiership players by the end of the day. It reminded me of that Burt Lancaster quote from the film the field of dreams 'We often don't recognise the most significant times in our life until they are over, we always think we will have another day, but so often, that was the only day'.
It was a beautiful summers day that the 22 players had been gifted with, in this their last match of camp. I was really looking forward to the game, as I had realised that this was the first match that I had attended, as every Sunday I would travel through to oxford and meet up with old friends from my study days. I was excited to see how good the boys football skills would be.
Aldous was still sitting first in the fantasy league, his twin was second only 2 points behind , which meant that if he played well and if team B won today then Aldous's brother may just beat him for the fantasy league title. Rocky was now in 4th

place and could still win it, but he would need to make up 6 points to reach Aldous.

The game started slowly and I could see that all the players were tense because of the high stakes that they were playing for. It was like watching a World Cup or Champions league final when the team tactics are very cagey, as no one wants to risk losing a goal first.

Both Aldous and Rocky were playing well and at this point in the game, both would have been favourites to get man of the match. Just before half-time Aldous scored by converting a cross delivered from rocky, into a solid header which whipped back into the net.

Apart from that fine piece of play, there hadn't really been anything else worthy of note in the first-half.

The second half was a different story, it started at a far higher pace and team B had came out with a bang. They scored with a free-kick within 5 minutes of the second half whistle. It was all still to play for. The game was now end to end excitement and it seemed like every player had now realised they only had another 45 minutes left in order to secure further employment. Then just as the 60th minute was being played, Aldous's twin brother Aaron playing for team B went down with severe cramp and signalled to frank the coach that he couldn't continue. I could see the scouts that were watching were disappointed as he had been playing well and may have just been doing enough to beat Aldous into first place. I could see Aldous unsportingly smile, as his twin was stretchered off the field by the physio coach. Frank blew the whistle and gathered everyone into the centre circle, including the other 5 coaches. The problem they now faced was that there were no substitutes at the summer camp as it was only designed to work with 22 players. Therefore, should they cancel the game?

Everyone agreed no, but Frank was a goalkeeper and felt that he could not play for one team against the other. The other coaches had worked with all the boys also and they felt it was a conflict of interest to play against some of their players on this big occasion. I could see Aldous with a malevolent wry smile on his face as he started pointing over to me and shouting 'why don't we give the Professor to the other team as he hasn't worked with any of them before'.

The 5 boys from my class all started laughing saying that it was a brilliant idea. I even heard them cheekily saying "Professor, there still plenty of time left in the game and who said that we are talking about football and remember professor you never lose in this game, you either win or you learn' (little wretches).

In fairness, I had to laugh at their mockery as it was quite funny and at least it showed that some of my little knowledge seeds had been stored in their minds.

Frank asked the other team 'if they would accept that and to my amazement they agreed as they just wanted to keep playing and finish the game'.

My 5 special boys in team A thought this was hilarious and couldn't believe their luck.

It was at that point, as they were falling about laughing at me putting on my football boots, that I noticed frank approaching them looking annoyed at their Childish mockery in front of the professional scouts which he had invited as special guests. I could see him gathering my 5 boys around him and in an instant all their faces changed to a grimace of surprise and fear, with whatever frank was saying to them.

Later he told me what he had said and it went something like this. He had said that "if they had more sense and cared about anyone else other than themselves, then at some point they would have asked Frank " how he had ever met me." His answer would have been to tell them that I was the best young player that he had ever graced a football pitch with. He played for England under 18's at international level and I played for Scotland. My nickname then was "Psycho" and I was one evil, brutal, tough little midfielder, who also had one hell of a temper and major anger issues. He had also witnessed my last ever game. It was a Scotland and England friendly warm-up match before the under-18's World Cup. I had been playing well in the game, but then got sent off unjustly after committing a fair tackle. However, I came back on the field 10 minutes later armed with a knife and I attacked both the player and the referee who had cost me my time in the game. Both were seriously harmed and I was imprisoned for 5 years and banned for life from ever playing professional football.

He had heard later that I was put in a self-development rehabilitation program in prison whilst also studying for a degree in sports psychology, and had eventually written a book on the subject. Finally, he told them, that he had heard that my son had recently committed suicide on a train and that is why he asked me to join the summercamp, as he felt it may have helped me to deal with this.

This was how Frank had came to know of me.

By the time I arrived on the pitch the boy's expressions had changed. I guess they had never assumed that young Alan, had also been a great player in this beautiful game at one point.

I can still remember that feeling again when the ball was passed to my feet. Just like riding a bike, you never forget it and within minutes I was running around like an 18 year old again, just as if the last 27 years had not happened. It was exhilarating and I was dribbling players and knocking them off the ball and within 10 minutes I had scored my first goal with a lovely volley into the top-right corner.

I turned and smiled at Aldous and then from out of nowhere this sudden adrenaline rush had made me start to do a strange goal celebration which had me slapping my knees and making vulgar tongue movements, just like some kind of drunk vulgar New Zealand rugby player.

I could hear music in my mind now " which sounded awfully like "you ain't see nothing yet by Bachman Turner overdrive. I was now getting more animated and more vocal in the game. Ten minutes later I had placed the ball in between the goalkeepers legs and into the back of the net. I could see the special 5 were not amused at my over-enthusiastic vulgar tongue celebration towards them. I could see them looking as if to say, "Where did this guy come from? Where has he been hiding for 12 weeks?'.

In the last minute of the game, then my hat-trick was completed with a lovely chip of the ball over their goalkeeper. I have to be honest and say that I was glad the game had ended, because I was getting a bit worried that my adrenaline levels were getting out of control and I may revert back to my past days of monkey-mind and beast behaviours.

It was me who won 'man of the match' and scored most points in the game (which I could tell Aldous wasn't happy about). I think some of the scouts may have signed me if it wasn't for my age (and of course my lifetime ban). Aldous won the overall fantasy football league summer camp title and I was happy for him as he deserved for his wonderful football skills.

I was also happy to hear that Rocky finished 4th, but was awarded the summer camp trophy for the 'most improved player'.

It had been a glorious summers day and I personally had a wonderful experience of travelling back in time to my youth days and feeling the energy of adrenaline in my legs again.

Frank had organised a barbecue before we all said our goodbyes, however I decided to leave early as goodbyes were never really my thing. I wished the 5 special boys all the best of luck with their future and hoped they would get signed for the team of their dreams.

I hugged each of them for the last time, and told them " boys, I hope that some of the techniques that I have shown you in the last 12 weeks , will help you to play your game better in the future and keep you moving forward on your map".

They laughed and repeated in unison with me, as I said my parting farewell words of wisdom to them which were; **"and who says that I am talking about football, but don't worry Boys, because you never lose in this game you only win or you learn.**

That was the last time I ever spoke to any of the boys again.

The next time I would meet them, they would all be retired players by then, and we would all be getting drunk at a Sports awards ceremony.

Chapter 20: The Journey has ended

'If you are going to play the game boy, you got to learn to play it right'
-Kenny rogers

And that was my story of how I met 'Rocky Richards', I told Alan.

I was surprised that he was still awake on the train and seemingly engrossed in my narrative, as I had felt that I had over-stretched on the detail of the summer camp and the sessions of my 12 week program. However, he told me that he found them really interesting and may try and remember a few of the techniques to help him move forward on his own journey, as he recently felt he had lost his way and was feeling hopeless about the future

He asked me what my 'special report' that I had given to Rocky tonight as a parting gift had contained with regards my future predictions for the 5 special boys.

S,o I proceeded to recall to him what I had written many years ago.

Here are the final prediction reports which I had composed for each of the boys along with my class scores and their summer camp fantasy football league scores.

Paulo the philosopher
Scored 90 points in class and was second out of the 5 boys.
Scored 90 points In The fantasy football league and was rated 7th out of the 22 boys at camp.

I predicted that Paulo would make it the professional game to a low sitting premiership team or a high situated 1st division team. He would be a solid player for the team but never make captain. He would play for just 2 or 3 clubs in his whole career.

He had the intelligence that at some point in his football career, he would start developing opportunities out with football. He would ultimately retire from football in his early 30's and go on to become a businessman in a topic related to sport or he would possibly go on to be a pundit in the game for the satellite TV companies. He would get married twice, once in his twenties and then again in his forties. He would have a couple of children with his first wife only.

His real life story was that he got signed up straight after summer camp for a 1st division team. This team routinely flitted between lower premiership and top 1st division. He retired at the age of 31 from football, but before retiring he was a director and partner in an events organising company, in which his area of speciality was organising sporting events like golf tournaments, formula 1 events and VIP football and rugby packages.
He occasionally was employed as a stand-in pundit for a small TV company when his original team were playing on the big screen. He is currently in his second marriage and has 2 children one boy and one girl to his first wife.

Paulo's twin-Pablo.
Pablo played scored 86 points and was 8th in camp,
He played in the 1st division for his entire career. He stayed with the same club for 20 years until his retirement. He now has a junior coaching role at the same club.
He has been married twice and has 1 child .

Anxious Ishmal
scored 80 points in class and was 3rd of the 5 boys.
Scored 74 points in the fantasy football league and was rated 14th out of the 22 boys at camp.

My prediction for Ishmal is that he would also play professional football but always in the 1st division and never the premiership. He would be a reliable player in his team but would never change team and the first major team that signed him would be the team he retires at. I predicted that Ishmal would retire early from football possibly with injury or scare of injury. He would then get involved in something financially rewarding but low risk like buying and selling or renting out properties .

He would get married only once and stay married. He would have 3 or more children. His children would all go to university.

His real life story is that he was not signed up after summer camp but would have to wait another 2 years before a low sitting 1st division club signed him. He stayed with this club until the day he retired at the age of 29 because of a recurrent hamstring injury. He won an FA cup and 1 first division title with his club as well as a first Division player of the year award.

He now successfully manages his own portfolio of commercial properties and is still married with 4 children. His eldest 2 children are currently studying medicine at Cambridge university and the youngest two children are still at high school.

Ishmals twin-Issac

Issac scored 65 points and was rated 16th at summercamp.
also played in the same team as Ishmal for many years. Although Issac retired earlier due to mental health issues of stress and depression. Issac retrained as sports physiotherapist. He never married and has no children.

Lennon the Joker

Scored 48 points in class and was 4th out of the 5 boys.
Scored 77 points in the fantasy football league and was 11th out of the 22 players at camp.

I predicted that Lennon would never make it as a professional football player as he would focus more on socialising too much with his local friends. He would ultimately never play football at the top level and would take up a more manual job in his local community. He would get married once but then his wife would divorce him and he would never repeat the process again. He would have 1 child, who he would see intermittently. He would end up with health issues mainly due to alcohol, diet and obesity and retire from a full-time working career in his 50's.

His real-life story was that he got signed straight after summer camp to a bottom table premiership team. However, after the divorce of his parents, he started drinking heavily the year after and after a few incidents of brawling outside pubs and clubs, the team dropped him and within 3 years of currently sliding further down into a bottle, he was playing semi-pro Sunday league football for beer vouchers. He did this for another 3 years before sustaining a major break in his right leg from the kind of horrendous tackle that you often see in Sunday league football and this ended his career at the age of 22. He then got a job as a painter and decorator with a local firm, where he spent a happy 30 years before his drinking and dietary habits eventually caught up with him and he had a heart attack which retired him from his work. He was married at the age of 21 when his wife was pregnant with their son. His wife and son left him 10 years later due to his excessive drinking. He never remarried and stays in a 1 bedroom flat on his own in the town centre. He does not have a great relationship with his only son.

Lennons twin-Lewis
Lewis scored 72 points at camp and was 12th at camp.
He also went off the rails when their parents divorced. Lewis didn't get offered a place with a football team after summer camp so he moved to wales with his mum and got involved in knife gangs and drugs. He has been in and out of jail for assault and petty crime ever since.
He has never been married and has 1 child.

Aldous the peacock
Scored 36 points in class. The lowest of the 5 boys.
Scored 105 points in the fantasy football league and was top of all the 22 players and duly won player of the camp.

I predicted that Aldous would get signed by a very good premiership team and he would initially fly like a real promising star, however he would do something to mess it up and the club would let him off with it and then he would repeat some bad decisions over again and the team would eventually get rid of him. I thought his performance in the game would peak about 20 and then his development and abilities would fall sharply each year due to many of his off-field lifestyle choices. I predicted by the age of 25 he would only be a star player in either a low 1st division or top 2nd division team but would stay here at this level in order to look good in front of local fans. Eventually, he would become more frustrated at his decline in footballing status, especially as he witnessed some of his previous teammates continue to develop their fortune and fame in the game. He would then move around many clubs on short term loans as each club would think they could change his behaviours. But, they would all be wrong. Aldous would still be playing professional football late into his 30's, probably at a 2nd division level. Mainly because he would need the money and the adoration of even a small amount of fans. Eventually, he would retire and a few of his old friends who had made it more successful in football would somehow nostalgically Pity him "for the player they remember that he could have Been", and they would probably try and help him out by giving him odd pieces of promotional work here and there and generally paying him over the odds as a favour to his pride.

He would never get married or admit to having any children and he would probably pass away in his late 40's or early 50's from eventually getting himself into too many sticky situations involving woman, alcohol, drugs, mixing with criminals or all of the above.

His real-life story was that he got signed up that final day of summer camp to a top 5 premiership team. He trained with the first team squad for 2 years and just at age of 19, as he was looking like he would soon be breaking through into the first squad, he was found guilty of the sexual assault of a girl in Spain.

His team had initially supported him though this, but a year later when he was convicted of seriously assaulting a police officer and numerous more charges of sexual assault on females then his club transferred him to a low 1st division team. He played very well in the 1st division for the next 2 years and there was talk of him getting a chance to return as a player into the premiership, however another hotel drunken sexual assault incident involving a minor, put an end to this and saw him loaned back out to a bottom table 2nd division team. He moved around clubs in the second division for the next 10 years until finally retiring in his mid 30's without ever winning a cup or even a medal in the game. He was then convicted on drug possession charges and spent the next 2 years in prison.

A few years after his release, he was found dead in his flat at the age of 44 due to a suspected heart attack from a cocktail of drink and drugs. He was never married and had no children (that he knew of). His girlfriend who had phoned summer camp, did not end up having the child.

Aldous's twin-Aaron

Aaron, who had finished second at summer camp with 102 points, never had the chance to play a competitive game as a professional football player. He was signed up for a mid-table premiership team, however at the age of 17 years old he was tragically killed in a high-speed car race with another promising young footballer when they were both drunk at the wheel of a car. They were both beginner drivers but were driving seriously advanced cars.

Resilient Rocky

Scored 112 points on the class league and was the top student of the 5 boys.

Scored 99 points in the fantasy football league and finished 4th out of the 22 players at camp.

I predicted that rocky would get signed up to a mid-table premiership team. He would continue to work hard on his fitness, his football and his leadership skills and by his early 20's he would gain his first cap for England. By his mid-20's he would be captain of his team and then he Would get offered a big money deal to move to a top premiership team. He would go on to captain this top team and help them win major competitions, as well as earn himself a large number of England caps along the way.

He would retire from playing top level football in his mid to late 30's after keeping himself in good shape and fitness. He would then go onto earn his coaching badges before finally managing a successful premiership team. He would get happily married and have 3 or more children.

His rea- life story was at end of summer camp, he was offered a place at a premiership team who were currently sitting bottom of the league. He signed for them and stayed for 10 years helping them to stay up and climb higher every year until they became a top 6 team. At the age of 26 he was offered a vast amount of money to sign for the 2nd best team in the premiership. Within 3 years he was captain and helped them to win the league and go onto to become one of the most successful British teams of all time. He won 5 premiership titles, 3 FA cups and 2 European cups, 3 player of the years and 1 European player of the year award and gained over 70 caps for England and captained them for 5 years.

He retired aged 36 and within 5 years he had his coaching badges and was managing a 1st division team.

By age 45, he had made a name as a good successful young coach after helping his first team gain promotion to the premiership and by age 50 he was now manager of the club he had helped as a player to win the premiership league title. He became one of the most successful British managers of his generation. He can still be seen in the Managing Directors box of his beloved club, that he played and managed. Fans still see him on TV providing commentary to the major sports channels during the big international competitions.

He is still married and has 4 children.

Rocky's twin-Richard
Scored 93 points at summer camp and was 5th of the 22 players.

He got signed and played for a 1st Division team for 10 years before deciding to give up football and pursue a career as a sports agent. Which he became very successful at. He is a divorcee with 1 child.

I finished by telling Alan, on the train 'that I sent my research report away for independent analysis and although the sample number of 5 boys was low, it does reveal that each of the 5 boys who had been in my class, performed better in the game than their twin, although their increase level of success did vary from boy to boy. Although I was happy with this result and my work did get published in some obscure behaviour change journal, I decided never to repeat the research again and no one else to date, has ever picked up on my work and took it forward with larger cohorts.

The next thing I heard, was the sound of a train announcement coming over the tannoy, that our next stop was a couple of minutes away. The young man was hurriedly
finishing playing the decision-enhancing computer game, and just as he stood up, he looked at me and I noticed a very different expression from the gambler, that I had first met on the train. I asked him if he now had a different hand which he wanted to keep playing the game with, or was he still ready to fold his hand in the game. He confidently stated he had a few more ideas of how to play a new game now and he thanked me for taking him off the subs bench and keeping him in the game.
I told him 'that he was welcome and that I hoped to hear great things one day about how he was playing the game of his life'. I sharply said back 'remember son, there is always more time left in the game to get another goal, and he quickly replied along with me **"and who says I am talking about football'**. We both laughed and he started to get off the train.
It felt like that final scene from good will hunting where the student steals the teacher's line.
Then, just before he stepped down onto the platform, I turned towards the boy and told him, 'that I should thank him instead', he looked back at me puzzled as he left the train and watched

me as the train drifted away'. As I looked down at my computer telling me it was game over and as I felt the large bottle of pills in my pocket and gazed at the bottle of wine next to me, I suddenly remembered the boys kind words and changed expression on his face from when I first met him to when he left the train. It made me realise, that I myself had been playing the game all wrong recently and thinking that I may stop, as it was no longer bringing me joy. But now I should play a new game instead, in order to focus on helping to keeping other players in the game.

I then closed my eyes, put my headphones on and played the song ' the gambler by Kenny rogers, and before I knew it, I was humming away to myself 'and in his final words I found an ace that I could keep, you got to know when to hold them, know when to fold them, know when to walk away and know when to run, you never count your money when your sitting at the table, there will be time enough for counting when the dealings done.........

Moving forward in our life Journey?

YOU ARE NOW HERE

YOU WANT TO BE HERE

YOU WERE HERE

Printed in Poland
by Amazon Fulfillment
Poland Sp. z o.o., Wrocław

53796437R00164